GOOD HOUSEKEEPING
STEP-BY-STEP COOKERY

D0311952

DESSERTS
AND PUDDINGS

Guild Publishing/Ebury Press
LONDON

This edition published 1984 by
Book Club Associates
By arrangement with Ebury Press

Consultant editor: Jeni Wright
Editor: Miren Lopategui
Design by Mike Leaman
Drawings by Kate Simunek
Photographs by James Jackson

Cover photograph: Profiteroles (page 44), Cherry Pie (page 108)

Filmset by Advanced Filmsetters (Glasgow) Ltd

Printed and bound in Italy by
New Interlitho, S.p.a., Milan

DESSERTS
AND PUDDINGS

CONTENTS

COOKERY NOTES

Follow either metric or imperial measures for the recipes in this book as they are not inter-changeable. Sets of spoon measures are available in both metric and imperial size to give accurate measurement of small quantities. All spoon measures are level unless otherwise stated. When measuring milk we have used the exact conversion of 568 ml (1 pint).

* Size 4 eggs should be used except when otherwise stated.

† Granulated sugar is used unless otherwise stated.

● Plain flour is used unless otherwise stated.

OVEN TEMPERATURE CHART

°C	°F	Gas mark
110	225	$\frac{1}{4}$
130	250	$\frac{1}{2}$
140	275	1
150	300	2
170	325	3
180	350	4
190	375	5
200	400	6
220	425	7
230	450	8
240	475	9

METRIC CONVERSION SCALE

LIQUID

Imperial	Exact conversion	Recommended ml
$\frac{1}{4}$ pint	142 ml	150 ml
$\frac{1}{2}$ pint	284 ml	300 ml
1 pint	568 ml	600 ml
$1\frac{1}{2}$ pints	851 ml	900 ml
$1\frac{3}{4}$ pints	992 ml	1 litre

For quantities of $1\frac{3}{4}$ pints and over, litres and fractions of a litre have been used.

SOLID

Imperial	Exact conversion	Recommended g
1 oz	28.35 g	25 g
2 oz	56.7 g	50 g
4 oz	113.4 g	100 g
8 oz	226.8 g	225 g
12 oz	340.2 g	350 g
14 oz	397.0 g	400 g
16 oz (1 lb)	453.6 g	450 g

1 kilogram (kg) equals 2.2 lb.

KEY TO SYMBOLS

1.00* Indicates minimum preparation and cooking times in hours and minutes. They do not include prepared items in the list of ingredients; calculated times apply only to the method. An asterisk * indicates extra time should be allowed, so check the note below symbols.

Chef's hats indicate degree of difficulty of a recipe: no hat means it is straightforward; one hat slightly more complicated; two hats indicates that it is for more advanced cooks.

£ Indicates a recipe which is good value for money; £ £ indicates an expensive recipe. No £ sign indicates an inexpensive recipe.

✳ Indicates that a recipe will freeze. If there is no symbol, the recipe is unsuitable for freezing. An asterisk * indicates special freezer instructions so check the note immediately below the symbols.

309 cals Indicates calories per serving, including any suggestions (e.g. cream, to serve) given in the ingredients.

DESSERTS AND PUDDINGS

Stuck for ideas when it comes to the pudding or dessert course? Look no further than this book—from everyday traditional puddings to wonderful dinner party desserts, it's literally packed full of new and exciting ideas, each recipe with its own fabulous full-colour photograph for you to feast your eyes on as well as your taste buds!

From the five separate chapters of recipes, you can choose a dessert or pudding to suit any occasion, and there are step-by-step illustrations for problem-free preparation. Pies, Tarts and Pastries includes recipes from all over the world; Dinner Party Desserts gives you lots of spectacular ideas, all easy to follow and many cook-ahead; Traditional and Everyday goes back to basics with all-time favourites; and Milk and Eggs has lots of luscious puds from two of the simplest of ingredients. To round off the recipe section there is Fruity Desserts, fresh and simple dishes which make the most of seasonal fruits.

At the back of the book there is a special section of Useful Information and Basic Recipes. Here you will find everything you need to help you when making puddings and desserts— advice on the best equipment to buy and use, information on ingredients—fruit, nuts, sugar, gelatine, chocolate, cream and eggs—plus tips on making pastry, meringues, pancakes and soufflés. And a selection of useful basic recipes which you'll find yourself turning to again and again.

Pies, Tarts and Pastries

Crisp, light pastry with sweet and tasty fillings make marvellous family puddings and dinner party desserts alike. And they have the added benefit of making a small amount of fruit go a long way—ideal for feeding a large gathering. Serve pies and puddings traditionally with a perfectly smooth homemade custard, or be wickedly extravagant and top with lashings of fresh whipped cream.

OLD ENGLISH APPLE PIE

| 1.10 | 🍴 | f | ✳ | 651 cals |

Serves 6

350 g (12 oz) shortcrust pastry (see page 155)

700 g (1½ lb) cooking apples

finely grated rind and juice of ½ a lemon

50 g (2 oz) granulated sugar

50 g (2 oz) dark soft brown sugar

15 ml (1 tbsp) plain flour

pinch of grated nutmeg

1.25 ml (¼ tsp) ground cinnamon

finely grated rind and juice of ½ an orange

50 g (2 oz) sultanas

15–25 g (½–1 oz) butter or margarine

caster sugar, to dredge

custard or pouring cream, to serve

1 Roll out two thirds of the pastry on a floured work surface and use to line a 23-cm (9-inch) pie dish. Refrigerate for 30 minutes with the remaining dough wrapped in cling film.

2 Meanwhile, peel and core the apples, then slice them thickly into a bowl of cold water to which the lemon juice has been added.

3 Mix the sugars, flour, nutmeg, cinnamon, lemon and orange rinds together and sprinkle a little of this on to the pastry lining.

4 Cover the bottom of the pastry lining with half of the sliced apples, then sprinkle with half the sultanas and half of the remaining sugar mixture. Repeat, using all the apples, sultanas and sugar.

5 Sprinkle the fruit with the orange juice and dot with butter or margarine.

6 Roll out the remaining pastry and use to cover the pie, sealing the edges well. Slash the top twice to let steam escape.

7 Use the pastry trimmings to make decorations for the pie. Brush the top of the pie with water and place on the decorations. Dredge with caster sugar.

8 Bake in the oven at 190°C (375°F) mark 5 for 35–40 minutes until the fruit is tender and the top is golden brown. Serve warm, with custard or cream.

OLD ENGLISH APPLE PIE

Spicy pies were popular in Elizabethan times. Cinnamon was always one of the favourite spices to use with apples, so too were nutmeg and ginger.

The Elizabethans often added wine to their sweet pies, with lemon or orange zest, and sometimes candied peel. To give your apple pies a real old-fashioned flavour, add one or two quinces instead of some of the apples.

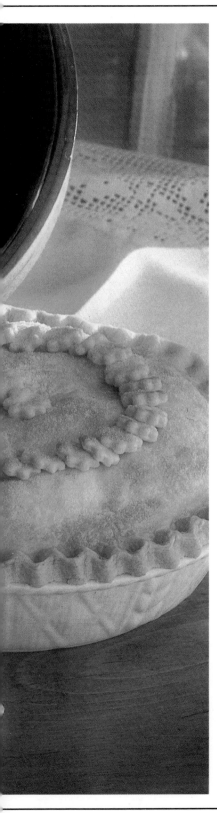

PEACH PIE

1.25* ⏲ £ £ 555 cals

* plus 15 minutes cooling

Serves 6

225 g (8 oz) plain flour

50 g (2 oz) walnuts, finely chopped

125 g (4 oz) softened butter or
    margarine, cut into pieces

75 g (3 oz) caster sugar

2 egg yolks

30 ml (2 tbsp) water

6 large peaches, about 900 g (2 lb)

1 egg white and caster sugar,
    to glaze

pouring cream, to serve

1 Place the flour on a clean, dry
work surface and sprinkle the
chopped walnuts over the top.
Make a well in the centre, then
place the butter in it with the
sugar, egg yolks and water.

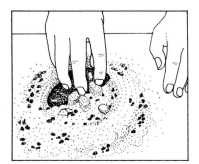

2 With the fingertips of one
hand only, pinch the well ingredients together until evenly
blended. Using a palette knife, cut
the flour into the well ingredients
and then knead the dough lightly
until just smooth.

3 Roll out two thirds on a
floured work surface and use
to line a 23-cm (9-inch) loose-
based fluted flan tin. Refrigerate
for 30 minutes.

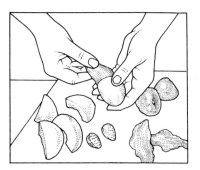

4 Meanwhile, quarter the
peaches and ease away from
the stone. Peel off the skins carefully and divide each quarter in
two lengthways.

5 Arrange the peaches in the flan
case. Roll out the remaining
pastry and use to cover the pie,
sealing the edges well. Make a
small hole in the centre to let
steam escape.

6 Bake in the oven, on a preheated baking sheet, at 200°C
(400°F) mark 6 for about 20–25
minutes or until it is just
beginning to brown.

7 Brush the top of the flan with
lightly beaten egg white and
dust with caster sugar. Return to
the oven for a further 10 minutes
or until well browned and crisp.
Cool for 15 minutes in the tin
before removing. Serve while still
slightly warm, with cream.

PUMPKIN PIE

1.25	£	670 cals

Serves 4

225 g (8 oz) shortcrust pastry (see page 155)

450 g (1 lb) pumpkin

2 eggs

100 g (4 oz) caster sugar

60 ml (4 tbsp) milk

pinch of grated nutmeg

pinch of ground ginger

10 ml (2 tsp) ground cinnamon

whipped cream, to serve

3 Steam the pieces of pumpkin between two plates over a pan of boiling water for 15–20 minutes until tender. Drain thoroughly, then mash well with a fork or purée in an electric blender or food processor.

4 Beat the eggs with the sugar. Add the pumpkin purée, the milk and spices. Blend well and pour into the pastry case.

5 Bake in the oven at 220°C (425°F) mark 7 for 15 minutes, then reduce the temperature to 180°C (350°F) mark 4 and bake for a further 30 minutes or until the filling is set. Serve warm, with whipped cream.

1 Roll out the pastry on a floured work surface and use to line a 20.5-cm (9-inch) flan case or deep pie plate; trim and decorate the edges. Refrigerate for about 30 minutes.

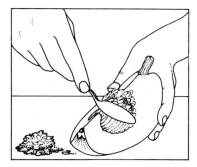

2 Meanwhile, cut the pumpkin into pieces, remove any seeds and 'cotton-woolly' inside part and cut off the outside skin.

MERINGUE MINCE TARTS

| 1.00 | 🍴 | £ £ | ✳ | 165 cals |

Makes 12

225 g (8 oz) shortcrust pastry (see page 155)

2 egg whites

100 g (4 oz) caster sugar

1 medium cooking apple

60 ml (12 tsp) mincemeat

30 ml (2 tbsp) orange-flavoured liqueur or brandy

finely grated rind of 1 orange

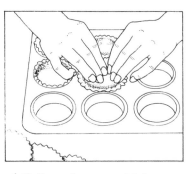

1 Roll out the pastry thinly on a floured work surface, then cut out twelve 7.5-cm (3-inch) rounds using a fluted pastry cutter. Use to line twelve deep patty tins. Brush the rounds with a little egg white. Refrigerate for 30 minutes. Prick the bases and bake blind in the oven at 200°C (400°F) mark 6 for 10–15 minutes until set.

2 Meanwhile, whisk the remaining egg whites in a clean, dry bowl until stiff, then beat in 15 ml (1 tbsp) of the sugar. Continue whisking until the meringue stands in stiff peaks, then fold in the rest of the sugar, reserving 10 ml (2 tsp).

3 Peel and core the apple, then grate into a bowl. Mix in the mincemeat, liqueur and rind.

4 Spoon the mincemeat mixture into the tarts, dividing it equally between them.

5 Top with the meringue, either by piping it with a large star nozzle or by spooning it on. Make sure there are no gaps between meringue and pastry. Sprinkle with the reserved sugar.

6 Bake in the oven at 190°C (375°F) mark 5 for 15–20 minutes until the meringue is crisp and golden. Serve the tarts warm or cold.

MERINGUE MINCE TARTS

Topping mince tarts with meringue instead of the usual pastry makes them somehow look more festive (especially if you pipe the icing on) and of course makes them much lighter to eat. The orange-flavoured liqueur or brandy in the recipe can be omitted, but try to use a good-quality mincemeat — brands containing alcohol are the nicest.

STRAWBERRY CUSTARD FLAN

| 0.35* | 🍴 | £ £ | 445–556 cals |

* plus 1 hour 10 minutes cooling and about 1½ hours chilling

Serves 6–8

175 g (6 oz) plain flour

125 g (4 oz) caster sugar

125 g (4 oz) butter or block margarine

3 eggs

40 g (1½ oz) cornflour

450 ml (¾ pint) milk

few drops of vanilla flavouring

350 g (12 oz) strawberries, hulled

pouring cream, to serve

1 Mix the flour with 25 g (1 oz) sugar in a bowl, then rub in the fat until the mixture resembles fine breadcrumbs. Bind to a soft dough with 1 egg. Knead lightly on a floured work surface until just smooth.

2 Roll out the pastry on a floured work surface and use to line a 23-cm (9-inch) flan dish. Refrigerate for 30 minutes. Prick the base of the flan and bake blind in the oven at 200°C (400°F) mark 6 for 20 minutes or until pale golden and cooked through. Cool in the dish for 30–40 minutes.

3 Mix the cornflour to a smooth paste with a little of the milk. Separate the remaining eggs and mix the egg yolks with the cornflour paste. Put the rest of the milk in a saucepan with the remaining sugar and the vanilla flavouring. Bring to the boil, then remove from the heat and pour in the cornflour mixture. Return to the boil, stirring, and boil for 2 minutes until thickened. Cover with damp greaseproof paper and cool for 30 minutes. (Whisk if necessary to remove lumps.)

4 Thinly slice the strawberries into the base of the flan, reserving a few for decoration. Whisk the egg whites until stiff and fold into the cold custard mixture. Smooth the custard mixture evenly over the strawberries. Refrigerate for 1 hour until set.

5 Serve the flan decorated with the reserved strawberry slices, preferably within 2 hours of completion. Serve with cream.

WALNUT MERINGUE TART

0.55* ⬜ f 475–658 cals

* plus 30 minutes chilling and 1 hour cooling

Serves 4–6

50 g (2 oz) butter or block margarine

175 g (6 oz) light soft brown sugar

1 egg yolk

100 g (4 oz) plain flour

2 egg whites

2.5 ml (½ tsp) vanilla flavouring

100 g (4 oz) walnuts, chopped

whipped cream, to serve

1 Melt the fat, cool for 5 minutes, then stir in 25 g (1 oz) of the sugar with the egg yolk and flour. Knead lightly, then press over the base and up the sides of a greased pie plate measuring 21.5 cm (8¼ inches) across the top. Refrigerate for 30 minutes.

2 Whisk the egg whites in a clean, dry bowl until stiff, but not dry. Gradually whisk in the remaining sugar, keeping mixture stiff. Add the vanilla flavouring with the last spoonful of sugar.

3 Fold in the chopped walnuts, then spoon into the pastry-lined pie plate.

4 Bake in the oven at 180°C (350°F) mark 4 for 30 minutes until the filling is well risen. Cool completely for 1 hour. As the meringue cools it will shrink and crack slightly.

5 Serve the walnut tart cold, cut in wedges, with whipped cream over the top.

TARTE FRANÇAISE

1.50* 🍴 ✳ 657 cals

* plus 30 minutes chilling and 10 minutes cooling

Serves 6

175 g (6 oz) plain flour
pinch of salt
175 g (6 oz) butter or block margarine
35 ml (7 tsp) caster sugar
1 egg yolk
45 ml (3 tbsp) water
900 g (2 lb) cooking apples
120 ml (9 tbsp) apricot jam
50 g (2 oz) granulated sugar
finely grated rind of $\frac{1}{2}$ a lemon
30 ml (2 tbsp) apple brandy or brandy
225 g (8 oz) eating apples
about 30 ml (2 tbsp) lemon juice

1 Put the flour and salt in a bowl. Rub in 125 g (4 oz) of the fat until the mixture resembles fine breadcrumbs; stir in 30 ml (6 tsp) of the caster sugar. Mix the egg yolk with 15 ml (1 tbsp) of the water and stir into the pastry mixture. Knead lightly on a floured work surface until just smooth.

2 Roll out the pastry and use to line a 20.5-cm (8-inch) flan ring placed on a baking sheet. Crimp the raised edges and refrigerate for 30 minutes.

3 Prick the base of the flan and bake blind in the oven at 180°C (350°F) mark 4 for 15–20 minutes until just set.

4 Cut the cooking apples into quarters, core and roughly chop the skin and flesh. Melt the remaining fat in a saucepan and add the apples with the remaining water. Cover the pan tightly and cook gently for about 15 minutes until soft and mushy.

5 Rub the apples through a sieve into a large clean pan. Add half the apricot jam with the granulated sugar, lemon rind and apple brandy. Cook over high heat for about 15 minutes stirring all the time, until all excess liquid has evaporated and the mixture is well reduced and thickened.

6 Spoon the thick apple purée into the flan case and smooth the surface. Peel, quarter, core and slice the eating apples very thinly. Arrange in an overlapping circle around the edge of the flan. Brush lightly with lemon juice; sprinkle with the remaining caster sugar.

7 Return the flan to the oven and bake for a further 25–30 minutes or until the pastry and apples are lightly coloured. Slide on to a serving plate and remove the flan ring. Cool for 10 minutes.

8 Gently warm the remaining jam with 15 ml (1 tbsp) lemon juice and, when well blended, sieve into a small bowl. While still warm, brush carefully over the top and sides of the flan until evenly glazed. Serve warm or chilled.

PEARS EN CHEMISE

1.00* ⊟ f 638 cals

* plus 30 minutes chilling

Serves 4

368-g (13-oz) packet frozen puff
 pastry, thawed

4 large dessert pears (e.g.
 Comice or Williams)

finely grated rind and juice of 1
 lemon

45 ml (9 tsp) redcurrant jelly

1 egg, beaten, to glaze

10 ml (2 tsp) caster sugar

pouring cream, to serve

1 Cut the pastry into four and
 roll out each piece on a lightly
floured work surface to an 18-cm
(7-inch) square.

2 Peel the pears and core them
 carefully from the bottom.
Leave the stalks on. Brush them
immediately with lemon juice to
prevent discoloration.

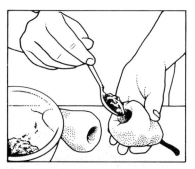

3 Mix together the lemon rind
 and half the redcurrant jelly.
Put 5 ml (1 tsp) into the cavity of
each pear, then stand the pears
upright in the centre of each
pastry square. Brush the edges of
the pastry with water.

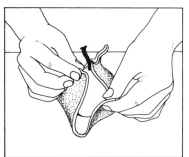

4 Bring the four corners of each
 square to the top of each pear
and press the edges to seal.

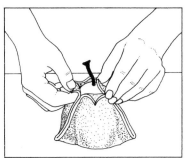

5 Fold back the four points to
 expose the stalk and allow
steam to escape. Stand the pears
on a dampened baking sheet and
refrigerate for 30 minutes.

6 Brush the pears all over with
 beaten egg and sprinkle with
the sugar. Bake in the oven at
220°C (425°F) mark 7 for 15–20
minutes until the pastry is crisp
and golden.

7 Warm the remaining redcurrant jelly and brush all over
the pastry. Serve warm, with
pouring cream.

BUTTERSCOTCH CREAM PIE

| 1.15* | 🍴 £ £ ❄ | 574 cals |

* plus 30 minutes chilling and 1 hour cooling

Serves 6

150 g (6 oz) plain flour
1.25 ml ($\frac{1}{4}$ tsp) salt
165 g (5$\frac{1}{2}$ oz) butter or block margarine
10 ml (2 tsp) caster sugar
5 egg yolks and 1 egg white
150 ml ($\frac{1}{4}$ pint) milk
170 g (6 oz) evaporated milk
50 g (2 oz) dark soft brown sugar
15 ml (1 tbsp) cornflour
300 ml (10 fl oz) double cream

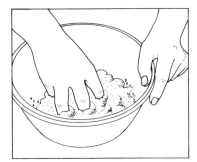

1 Put the flour into a bowl with half the salt. Add the 100 g (4 oz) fat in pieces and rub in with the fingertips until the mixture resembles fine breadcrumbs.

2 Stir in the sugar and 1 egg yolk and draw the dough together to form a ball. Add a few drops of cold water if the dough is too dry.

3 Press the dough gently into a 20.5-cm (8-inch) loose-bottomed fluted flan tin or ring placed on a baking sheet. Refrigerate for 30 minutes.

4 Prick the base of the pastry case and bake blind in the oven at 200°C (400°F) mark 6 for 10 minutes. Remove the foil and beans, brush the pastry with the egg white, then return to the oven and bake for a further 10 minutes until crisp and lightly coloured. Leave to cool.

5 Meanwhile, make the filling. Put the milk and evaporated milk in a saucepan and scald by bringing up to boiling point. Put the brown sugar, cornflour, remaining butter, egg yolks and salt in a heavy-based saucepan. Heat gently until the butter has melted and sugar dissolved, then gradually stir in the scalded milks. Stir well until heated through.

6 Cook over gentle heat, whisking constantly until the custard is thick. (Don't worry if the mixture is lumpy at first—keep whisking vigorously with a balloon whisk and it will become smooth.)

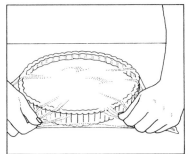

7 Remove from the heat and cool slightly, then pour into the baked pastry case. Cover the surface of the butterscotch cream closely with cling film (to prevent a skin forming) and leave for about 1 hour until completely cold.

8 To serve, whip the cream until stiff, then pipe on top of pie. Chill until serving time.

CHERRY STRUDEL

3.00	🍴 🍴 £ £ ✳

523–784 cals

Serves 4–6

225 g (8 oz) plus 15–30 ml (1–2 tbsp) plain flour

2.5 ml ($\frac{1}{2}$ tsp) salt

1 egg, lightly beaten

30 ml (2 tbsp) vegetable oil

60 ml (4 tbsp) lukewarm water

700 g (1$\frac{1}{2}$ lb) ripe black cherries, pitted and very finely chopped

45 ml (3 tbsp) black cherry jam

30 ml (2 tbsp) kirsch

75 g (3 oz) caster sugar

2.5 ml ($\frac{1}{2}$ tsp) ground cinnamon

40 g (1$\frac{1}{2}$ oz) butter, melted

100 g (4 oz) ground almonds

icing sugar, to dredge

1 Put the 225 g (8 oz) flour and salt into a large mixing bowl, make a well in the centre and pour in the egg and oil. Add the water gradually, stirring with a fork to make a soft, sticky dough.

2 Work the dough in the bowl until it leaves the sides, turn it out on to a lightly floured surface and knead for 15 minutes. Form into a ball, place on a cloth and cover with a warmed bowl. Leave the dough to 'rest' in a warm place for about 1 hour.

3 In a bowl, thoroughly mix together the cherries, the cherry jam, the kirsch, sugar and ground cinnamon.

4 Warm a rolling pin. Spread a clean cotton cloth on the table and sprinkle lightly with 15–30 ml (1–2 tbsp) flour. Place the dough on the cloth and roll out into a rectangle about 0.3 cm ($\frac{1}{8}$ inch) thick, lifting and turning it to prevent it sticking to the cloth.

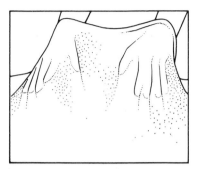

5 Gently stretch the dough, working from the centre to the outside and using the backs of the hands until it is paper-thin. Trim the edges to form a rectangle about 68 × 60 cm (27 × 24 in). Leave the strudel dough on the cloth to dry and 'rest' for about 15 minutes before filling and rolling.

6 Position the dough with one of the long sides towards you, brush with half the melted butter and sprinkle with ground almonds. Spread the cherry mixture over the dough, leaving a 5-cm (2-inch) border uncovered all round the edge.

MAKING STRUDEL DOUGH

Elasticity is the key word when it comes to making strudel pastry.

Strudel dough is unique in that it is exceptionally strong; it is not difficult to make as long as the instructions given in the method are followed. The 15-minute kneading in step 2 is vitally important to develop the gluten in the flour and so make the dough elastic and strong enough to be rolled so thin.

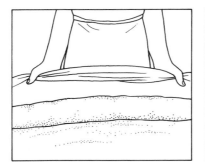

7 Fold the pastry edges over the cherry mixture, towards the centre. Lift the corners of the cloth nearest to you over the pastry, causing the strudel to roll up, but stop after each turn in order to pat into shape and to keep the roll even.

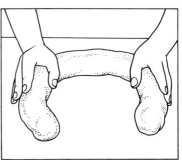

8 Form the roll into a horseshoe shape, brush it with the rest of the melted butter and slide it on to a buttered baking sheet. Bake in the oven at 190°C (375°F) mark 5 for about 40 minutes or until golden brown. Dredge the strudel with icing sugar. Serve warm cut into 4–6 slices.

FUDGY NUT PIE

1.35	£ £ ✳	607 cals*

* excluding ice cream; 702 cals with 50 g (2 oz) ice cream

Serves 8

225 g (8 oz) shortcrust pastry (see page 155)

50 g (2 oz) plain chocolate, broken into small pieces

50 g (2 oz) butter or margarine

175 g (6 oz) caster sugar

75 g (3 oz) light soft brown sugar

100 ml (4 fl oz) milk

75 g (3 oz) corn syrup or golden syrup

5 ml (1 tsp) vanilla flavouring

1.25 ml (¼ tsp) salt

3 eggs

100 g (4 oz) chopped mixed nuts

icing sugar, to decorate

vanilla ice cream, to serve

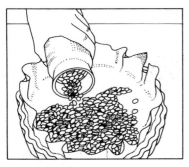

1 Roll out the pastry on a floured work surface and use to line a 23-cm (9-inch) flan dish or fluted flan ring placed on a baking sheet. Bake blind in the oven at 200°C (400°F) mark 6 for 10–15 minutes until set. Set aside to cool.

2 While the pastry case is cooling, put the chocolate and fat in a large heatproof bowl standing over a pan of simmering water. Heat gently until melted.

3 Remove bowl from the pan and add the remaining ingredients, except for the chopped nuts. Beat with a wooden spoon until well mixed, then stir in the nuts.

4 Pour the filling into the pastry case and bake in the oven at 180°C (350°F) mark 4 for 45–60 minutes or until puffy and golden. Dredge with icing sugar. Serve hot or cold with ice cream.

FUDGY NUT PIE

Rich and nutty, this pie has a definite 'American' flavour. Corn syrup is a popular ingredient in American pies and desserts. A by-product of sweetcorn, it is similar to golden syrup but has a thinner consistency and lighter flavour. Look for it in delicatessens and large supermarkets if you want to give your pie an authentic flavour. Americans use unsweetened 'baker's' chocolate for dessert making and baking, but this is very difficult to obtain outside the U.S. Instead, use a good-quality plain chocolate: French and Belgian varieties are the least sweet and have good melting qualities.

Dinner Party Desserts

A dinner party is the one occasion when you can really go to town with the dessert course. Show off your culinary skills and create something really special which is sure to impress your guests. Chocolate, cream, liqueur, fresh fruit, meringue and ice cream can all be used with gay abandon—and they're all here in this chapter to tempt your tastebuds.

CRÊPES SUZETTE

0.40* ☐ £ £ ❄*

370–554 cals

* not including making the pancake batter; freeze cooked crêpes only

Serves 4–6

105 ml (7 tbsp) orange-flavoured liqueur

pancake batter made with 300 ml (½ pint) milk (see page 151)

100 g (4 oz) unsalted butter

100 g (4 oz) caster sugar

finely grated rind and juice of 1 large orange

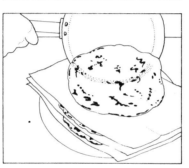

1 Stir 15 ml (1 tbsp) liqueur into the batter, then make 8–12 pancakes in the usual way (see page 151). Slide each crêpe out of the pan on to a warm plate and stack with greaseproof paper in between.

2 To serve, heat the butter and sugar together in a large, heavy-based frying pan until thick and syrupy. Add 30 ml (2 tbsp) liqueur and the orange rind and juice and heat through.

3 Fold the crêpes into triangle shapes by folding each one in half, then in half again. Place them in the frying pan and spoon over the sauce so that they become evenly coated.

4 Heat the remaining liqueur gently in a ladle or separate small pan. Transfer the crêpes and sauce to a warmed serving dish, pour over the warmed liqueur and set alight. Carry the crêpes to the table immediately, while they are still flaming.

CRÊPES SUZETTE

A classic French dessert; with its spectacular flambéed finish, crêpes Suzette is just perfect for a special dinner party. Traditionally flambéed at the table in a copper chafing dish in restaurants specialising in *haute cuisine*, the crêpes can look just as good at home carried flaming to the table on a silver or fine china plate.

This recipe uses orange juice and orange-flavoured liqueur, although the original classic recipe contained mandarin juice and orange liqueur, both in the crêpe batter and in the filling. If you wish to make this classic version rather than our more modern variation, try the following: Add 5 ml (1 tsp) each mandarin juice and orange-flavoured liqueur to the pancake batter before frying. Make a filling by creaming together 50 g (2 oz) each of unsalted butter and caster sugar. Work in the finely grated rind and juice of 1 mandarin orange and 15 ml (1 tbsp) orange-flavoured liqueur. When the crêpes are cooked, spread them with filling, fold into triangles, place in the serving dish and flambé with more liqueur.

BAKED ALASKA

0.30*	🥄 £	245–326 cals

* plus 2 hours macerating

Serves 6–8

225 g (8 oz) fresh or frozen
   raspberries

30 ml (2 tbsp) orange-flavoured
   liqueur

20.5-cm (8-inch) cooked sponge
   flan case (see page 155)

4 egg whites, at room temperature

175 g (6 oz) caster sugar

483-ml (17-fl oz) block vanilla ice
   cream

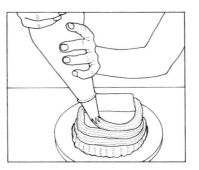

1 Place the fresh or frozen raspberries on a shallow dish and sprinkle over the liqueur. Cover and leave to macerate for 2 hours, turning occasionally.

2 Place the sponge flan on a large ovenproof serving dish and spoon the raspberries and juice into the centre.

3 Whisk the 4 egg whites in a clean, dry bowl until stiff, but not dry. Add 20 ml (4 tsp) caster sugar and whisk again, keeping the mixture stiff. Sprinkle over the remaining sugar and fold through gently.

4 Fit a piping bag with a large star nozzle and fill with the meringue mixture.

5 Place the block of ice cream on top of the raspberries, then immediately pipe the meringue on top. Start from the sponge base and pipe the meringue around and over the ice cream until it is completely covered, leaving no gaps.

6 Immediately place the completed Alaska in a preheated oven and bake at 230°C (450°F) mark 8 for 3–4 minutes. At this stage the meringue should be nicely tinged with brown. Watch the meringue carefully as it burns easily. Do not overcook or the ice cream will become too soft. Serve at once, before the ice cream begins to melt.

BAKED ALASKA

A spectacular dessert for a special dinner party, the recipe for baked Alaska originated in the U.S., where it is also sometimes called Norwegian Omelet or *omelette norvégienne* in French. Although impressive to serve, Baked Alaska is in fact surprisingly easy to make; the essential thing is to allow yourself unhurried time in the kitchen before serving—Baked Alaska cannot be kept waiting once it is cooked!

To help things run smoothly, prepare as much as you can before your dinner party starts. Make the sponge case and top with the fruit up to the end of stage 2, then whisk the meringue until stiff as in stage 3. Once your guests have finished their main course, you will only have to pop the ice cream on top of the fruit, pipe over the meringue and bake the dessert in the oven for a few minutes.

PETITS POTS AU CHOCOLAT

1.45*	£	410 cals

* plus 1 hour cooling

Serves 6

15 ml (1 tbsp) coffee beans

3 egg yolks

1 egg

75 g (3 oz) caster sugar

700 ml (1¼ pints) milk and single cream mixed

75 g (3 oz) plain chocolate

150 ml (5 fl oz) whipping cream and coffee dragées, to decorate

1 Toast the coffee beans under a moderate grill for a few minutes, then set aside.

2 Beat together the egg yolks, whole egg and sugar until the mixture is very pale.

3 Place the milk, cream and coffee beans in a saucepan and bring to the boil.

4 Strain the hot milk on to the egg mixture, stirring all the time. Discard the coffee beans.

5 Return the mixture to the saucepan, break up the chocolate and add to the pan. Stir over gentle heat (do not boil) for about 5 minutes until the chocolate has almost melted and mixture is *slightly* thickened. Whisk lightly until evenly blended.

6 Stand six individual 150-ml (¼-pint) ramekin dishes or custard pots in a roasting tin, then pour in enough hot water to come halfway up the sides of the dishes. Pour the custard mixture slowly into the dishes, dividing it equally between them. Cover, then bake in the oven at 150°C (300°F) mark 2 for 1–1¼ hours or until the custard is lightly set.

7 Leave to cool. To serve, whip the cream and spoon into a piping bag fitted with a large star nozzle. Pipe a whirl on top and decorate with coffee dragées.

CHOCOLATE

These little chocolate pots rely heavily on the flavour of the chocolate used in their making. So it is essential to use a good-quality chocolate. Plain chocolate is specified because it has better melting qualities than milk chocolate, and it also contains rather less sugar. For best results, look for French and Belgian plain cooking chocolates in delicatessens and specialist supermarkets.

NÈGRE EN CHEMISE

0.30* 📖 £ £ ✳ 854 cals

* plus 2–3 hours setting

Serves 8

350 g (12 oz) plain chocolate, broken into pieces

100 ml (4 fl oz) water

75 g (3 oz) butter or margarine

100 g (4 oz) praline, crushed (see page 142)

15 ml (1 tbsp) brandy

450 ml (15 fl oz) double cream

chocolate circles, to decorate (see page 147)

1 Put the chocolate and water in a heatproof bowl standing over a pan of simmering water. Heat gently until melted. Remove bowl from the pan and cool slightly.

2 Meanwhile, cream the fat in a bowl until pale. Add the melted chocolate and gradually beat in praline. Stir in brandy.

3 Lightly whip the cream and fold half into the chocolate mixture. Turn the mixture into a lightly oiled 900-ml (1½-pint) basin and refrigerate for 2–3 hours until set.

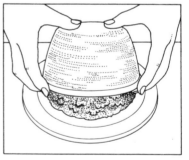

4 To serve. Quickly dip the basin into hot water, place a serving plate on top and invert. Lift off the basin.

5 Fill a piping bag, fitted with a large star nozzle, with the remaining cream and pipe around the base of the dessert. Decorate with chocolate circles. Refrigerate until serving time.

ICED ZABAGLIONE

0.25* ☐ £ 366 cals

* plus 30 minutes cooling and 2 hours freezing

Serves 6

4 egg yolks

65 g (2½ oz) caster sugar

100 ml (4 fl oz) marsala

200 ml (7 fl oz) double cream

30 ml (2 tbsp) iced water

30 ml (2 tbsp) icing sugar

orange shreds, to decorate

sponge fingers, to serve

1 Put the egg yolks and sugar in a large bowl. Beat together, add the marsala and beat again.

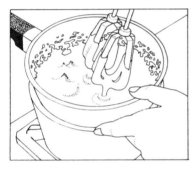

2 Place the bowl over a saucepan of simmering water and heat gently, whisking the mixture until it is very thick and creamy and forms soft peaks. Remove the bowl from the heat and leave to cool for about 30 minutes.

3 Place the cream and water in a bowl and sift in the icing sugar. Whisk until stiff then fold into the cooled egg mixture. Chill in the refrigerator for about 2 hours until firm.

4 Spoon the iced zabaglione into six individual glasses, decorate with orange shreds and serve with sponge fingers handed separately.

SNOWCAP ICED PUDDING

| 1.15* | 🥄 | £ £ | ✳ | 303–405 cals |

* plus 2 hours setting and overnight
freezing

Serves 6–8

150 ml ($\frac{1}{4}$ pint) kirsch

60 ml (4 tbsp) water

about 15 sponge fingers

450 ml ($\frac{3}{4}$ pint) chocolate chip ice
cream

225 g (8 oz) ripe cherries, pitted and
roughly chopped

450 ml ($\frac{3}{4}$ pint) vanilla ice cream

150 ml (5 fl oz) double cream

1 Cut out a circle of greaseproof
paper and use it to line the
base of a 1.1-litre (2$\frac{1}{2}$-pint)
pudding basin.

2 Mix the kirsch with the water
and dip the sponge fingers one
at a time into the mixture. Use to
line the sides of the pudding basin,
trimming them to fit so that there
are no gaps in between. Fill the
base of the basin with leftover
pieces of sponge. Refrigerate for
15 minutes.

3 Stir any remaining kirsch
liquid into the chocolate ice
cream and mash the ice cream well
with a fork to soften it slightly and
make it smooth.

4 Spoon the chocolate ice cream
into the basin and work it up
the sides of the sponge fingers to
the top of the basin so that it
forms an even layer. Freeze for
about 2 hours until firm.

5 Mix the cherries into the
vanilla ice cream and mash
well with a fork as in step 3.

6 Spoon the vanilla ice cream
into the centre of the basin and
smooth it over the top so that it
covers the chocolate ice cream and
the sponge fingers. Cover with foil
and freeze overnight.

7 To serve, whip the cream until
it will just hold its shape. Run
a knife around the inside of the
basin, then turn the ice cream out
on to a serving plate.

8 Spoon the cream over the top
and let it just start to run
down the sides, then freeze immediately for about 15 minutes or
until the cream has frozen solid.
Serve straight from the freezer.

CHARLOTTE RUSSE

| 1.35* | ⎕ ⎕ £ | 447 cals |

* plus 50 minutes cooling and 4 hours setting

Serves 6

135-g (4¾-oz) packet lemon jelly, broken into squares

about 450 ml (¾ pint) boiling water

45 ml (3 tbsp) lemon juice

2 glacé cherries, quartered

piece of angelica, cut into triangles

300 ml (½ pint) milk

1 vanilla pod

45 ml (3 tbsp) water

15 ml (3 tsp) gelatine

3 egg yolks

45 ml (3 tbsp) caster sugar

about 18 sponge fingers

300 ml (10 fl oz) whipping cream

1 Dissolve the jelly in a measuring jug, according to the packet instructions, using the lemon juice and enough boiling water to make 600 ml (1 pint). Cool for 20 minutes. Spoon a thin covering of cool jelly into the base of a 1.1-litre (2-pint) charlotte tin; refrigerate for about 20 minutes or until set.

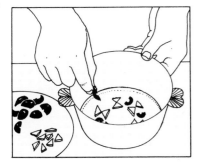

2 When set, arrange the cherry quarters and angelica triangles on top. Carefully spoon over cool liquid jelly to a depth of about 2.5 cm (1 inch). Refrigerate for about 30 minutes to set, together with the remaining jelly.

3 Bring the milk slowly to the boil with the vanilla pod; take off the heat, cover and leave to infuse for at least 10 minutes. Put the water in a small bowl and sprinkle in the gelatine. Stand the bowl over a saucepan of hot water and heat gently until dissolved. Remove the bowl from the water and set aside to cool slightly.

4 Using a wooden spoon, beat together the egg yolks and sugar until well mixed, then stir in the strained milk. Return to the pan and cook gently, stirring all the time until the custard is thick enough to just coat the back of the spoon—do *not* boil. Pour into a large bowl, stir in the gelatine and allow to cool for 30 minutes.

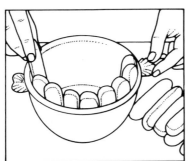

5 Trim the sponge fingers so that they just fit the tin; reserve the trimmings. Stand the fingers closely together, sugar side out, around the edge of the tin.

6 Lightly whip the cream and stir into the cool custard. Place the bowl in a roasting tin. Pour in enough iced water to come halfway up its sides. Stir occasionally for about 10 minutes until the custard is on the point of setting and has a *thick* pouring consistency. Pour gently into the lined mould without disturbing the sponge fingers.

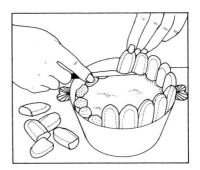

7 Trim the sponge fingers level with the custard. Lay the trimmings together with the reserved trimmings on top of the custard. Cover with cling film and refrigerate for at least 3 hours to set.

8 To turn out, using fingertips, ease the sponge fingers away from the tin, then tilt it slightly to allow an airlock to form between the two. Dip the base of the tin in hot water for about 5 seconds only—to loosen the jelly. Invert the pudding on to a damp plate, shake tin gently, then ease it carefully off the finished charlotte.

9 Loosen the remaining set jelly by dipping the jug in hot water for a few seconds only. Turn out on to a board lined with damp greaseproof paper. Moisten a large knife and chop the jelly into small pieces. Spoon the jelly around the charlotte russe.

CHARLOTTE RUSSE

A classic French dessert, this charlotte Russe (Russian charlotte) is made with a filling of *crème bavarois*—a rich vanilla-flavoured egg custard. Sometimes the custard is flavoured with chocolate, almond-flavoured liqueur or kirsch. Fresh raspberries can also be added when they are in season.

TIPSY CAKE

0.30* £ ✳ 690 cals

* plus overnight refrigeration

Serves 6

700 g (1½ lb) stale madeira or
   sponge cake

175 ml (6 fl oz) sherry

100 g (4 oz) strawberry or sieved
   raspberry jam

75 g (3 oz) walnuts, chopped

150 ml (5 fl oz) whipping cream

crystallised violets and mimosa
   balls, to decorate

1 Crumble the cake into a bowl.
Add the sherry, jam and
walnuts and mix well.

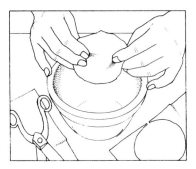

2 Line the base of a 900-ml (1½-
pint) pudding basin with a
circle of greaseproof paper.

3 Spoon the mixture into the
pudding basin, cover with
greaseproof paper and place heavy
weights on top. Chill in the
refrigerator overnight.

4 The next day, remove the
weights, turn the cake out on
to a serving plate and remove the
greaseproof paper circle.

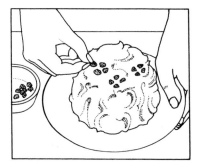

5 Whip the cream until standing
in soft peaks, then swirl over
the cake to cover it completely.
Decorate with crystallised violets
and mimosa balls. Refrigerate
until serving time.

TIPSY CAKE

A kind of old-fashioned trifle,
tipsy cake is rich and very
boozy. Originally made with
Madeira wine and brandy rather
than the sherry used here, it was
also sometimes covered in a thick
egg custard before being
smothered with cream. The
crystallised violets used to decorate this pretty dessert look very
delicate. Years ago they would
have used fresh flowers to decorate a tipsy cake for a special
occasion—and you can do the
same today if you wish. Pale
green pistachio nuts or toasted
blanched almonds can also be
used for decoration; either would
make a striking contrast with the
flowers and cream.

   If you are making tipsy cake
for a special occasion—it makes
an eye-catching table centrepiece
for a buffet party—it can be
made up to the end of step 3
several days beforehand and
stored in the refrigerator.

COFFEENUT ICE CREAM

| 0.40* | ⊟ | £ £ | ✳ | 669 cals |

* plus at least 6 hours freezing and 30 minutes softening

Serves 4

100 g (4 oz) shelled hazelnuts

50 ml (2 tbsp plus 4 tsp) coffee-flavoured liqueur

15 ml (1 tbsp) coffee and chicory essence

300 ml (10 fl oz) double cream

300 ml (10 fl oz) single cream

75 g (3 oz) icing sugar, sifted

1 Toast the hazelnuts under the grill for a few minutes, shaking the grill pan constantly so that the nuts brown evenly.

2 Tip the nuts into a clean tea-towel and rub to remove the skins. Chop finely.

3 Mix 30 ml (2 tbsp) coffee liqueur and the essence together in a bowl. Stir in the chopped nuts, reserving a few for decoration.

4 In a separate bowl, whip the creams and icing sugar together until thick. Fold in the nut mixture, then turn into a shallow freezerproof container. Freeze for 2 hours until ice crystals form around the edge of the ice cream.

5 Turn the ice cream into a bowl and beat thoroughly for a few minutes to break up the ice crystals. Return to the freezer container, cover and freeze for at least 4 hours, preferably overnight (to allow enough time for the flavours to develop).

6 To serve, transfer the ice cream to the refrigerator for 30 minutes to soften slightly, then scoop into individual glasses. Spoon 5 ml (1 tsp) coffee liqueur over each serving and sprinkle with the remaining nuts. Serve immediately.

ICE CREAM MAKERS

It is always satisfying to make your own ice cream, but sometimes the texture is disappointing because large ice crystals have formed in the mixture due to insufficient beating. Electric ice cream makers help enormously with this problem: they are not very expensive and are well worth buying if you like to make ice cream for occasions such as dinner parties when everything needs to be as near perfect as possible. The mixture is placed in the machine, which is then put into the freezer and switched on (the cable is flat so that the freezer door can close safely on it). Paddles churn the mixture continuously until the mixture is thick, creamy and velvety smooth—a consistency that is almost impossible to obtain when beating by hand.

BANANA CHEESECAKE

0.40* 🗋 £ £ ✳*

428–570 cals

* plus 3–4 hours chilling; freeze after step 5. Defrost in refrigerator overnight, then continue with step 6.

Serves 6–8

225 g (8 oz) ginger biscuits

100 g (4 oz) unsalted butter, melted and cooled

225 g (8 oz) full fat soft cheese

142-ml (5-fl oz) carton soured cream

3 bananas

30 ml (2 tbsp) clear honey

15 ml (1 tbsp) chopped preserved ginger (with syrup)

15 ml (3 tsp) gelatine

60 ml (4 tbsp) lemon juice

banana slices and preserved ginger slices, to decorate

1 Make the biscuit crust. Crush the biscuits finely in a bowl with the end of a rolling pin. Stir in the melted butter.

2 Press the mixture over the base of a 20.5-cm (8-inch) springform tin or deep cake tin with a removable base. Chill in the refrigerator for about 30 minutes.

3 Meanwhile, make the filling. Beat the cheese and cream together until well mixed. Peel and mash the bananas, then beat into the cheese mixture with the honey and ginger.

4 Sprinkle the gelatine over the lemon juice in a small heatproof bowl. Stand the bowl over a saucepan of hot water and heat gently until dissolved.

5 Stir the dissolved gelatine slowly into the cheesecake mixture, then spoon into the biscuit-lined tin. Chill in the refrigerator for about 3–4 hours until the mixture is set.

6 To serve, remove the cheesecake carefully from the tin and place on a serving plate. Decorate around the edge with banana and ginger slices. Serve as soon as possible or the banana will discolour.

───── VARIATION ─────

The flavours of banana and ginger go very well together, but you can ring the changes by using chocolate digestive biscuits for the base of this cheesecake instead of ginger biscuits, and omitting the preserved ginger from the filling. Decorate the top with banana slices arranged alternately with chocolate buttons.

PROFITEROLES

Pictured on cover

| 1.10* | ⏣ | £ | ❄* | 685 cals |

* plus 20 minutes cooling; freeze after step 5. Defrost in refrigerator overnight, then continue from step 6.

Serves 4

50 g (2 oz) butter or margarine

150 ml (¼ pint) water

65 g (2½ oz) plain flour

2 eggs, lightly beaten

150 ml (5 fl oz) double cream

icing sugar, to dredge

175 g (6 oz) plain chocolate, broken into pieces

large knob of butter

45 ml (3 tbsp) milk

45 ml (3 tbsp) golden syrup

1 Make the choux pastry. Put the fat and water in a saucepan. Heat gently until the fat has melted, then bring to the boil. Remove the pan from the heat.

2 Tip the flour all at once into the hot liquid. Beat thoroughly with a wooden spoon, then return the pan to the heat.

3 Continue beating the mixture until it is smooth and forms a ball in the centre of the pan. (Take care not to over-beat or the mixture will become fatty.) Remove from the heat and leave the mixture to cool for a minute or two.

4 Beat in the egg, a little at a time, adding only just enough to give a piping consistency. It is important to beat the mixture vigorously at this stage to trap in as much air as possible. A hand-held electric mixer is ideal for this purpose. Continue beating until the mixture develops a sheen.

5 Dampen the surface of two or three baking sheets with water. Fill a piping bag fitted with a medium plain nozzle with the choux pastry and pipe small balls, about the size of walnuts, on to the baking sheets.

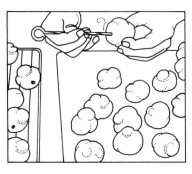

6 Bake in the oven at 220°C (425°F) mark 6 for 25–30 minutes until crisp. Make a hole in the bottom of each profiterole to release the steam, and leave to cool on a wire rack for 20 minutes.

7 Whip the cream until stiff. Fill a piping bag fitted with a medium plain nozzle with the cream, and use to fill the profiteroles.

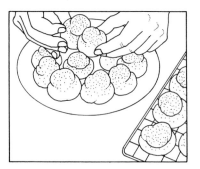

8 Dredge with icing sugar and pile the profiteroles into a pyramid shape.

9 To make the chocolate sauce, put the chocolate in a small bowl with the butter. Add the milk and syrup. Stand the bowl over a pan of warm water and heat gently, stirring, until the chocolate has melted and the sauce is warm.

10 Beat well, then pour a little chocolate sauce over the profiteroles and serve the rest separately. Serve immediately.

PROFITEROLES

A pyramid of luscious, cream-filled profiteroles coated in a rich chocolate sauce is an all-time favourite dinner party dessert. Take care when making choux pastry that the dough does not become too fatty through over-beating, as this will result in heavy-textured profiteroles. For the same reason, when adding the eggs in stage 4, watch the consistency of the dough carefully. Eggs vary in size even within their grade, and flour absorbs different amounts of liquid depending on its freshness and the temperature of the room you are working in. If the dough begins to feel slack, you do not need to add all of the beaten egg.

ORANGES EN SURPRISE

| 0.50* | £ £ ✳ | 392 cals |

* plus at least 4 hours (preferably overnight) freezing

Serves 6

6 large oranges

300 ml (10 fl oz) double cream

50 g (2 oz) icing sugar

90 ml (6 tbsp) orange-flavoured liqueur

90 ml (6 tbsp) chunky orange marmalade

fresh bay leaves or chocolate rose leaves, to decorate (optional)

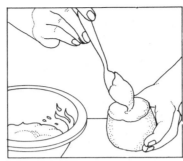

3 Spoon the cream mixture into the orange shells, mounding it up so that it protrudes over the top. Freeze for at least 4 hours, preferably overnight (to allow the flavours to develop). Serve straight from the freezer, decorated with reserved orange lids, bay or chocolate rose leaves.

1 Cut a slice off the top of each orange and reserve. Scoop out all the flesh, pips and juice from the oranges and discard (the juice can be used for drinking or in other recipes). Wash, then dry thoroughly. Set aside.

2 Whip the cream with the icing sugar until standing in stiff peaks. Mix together the liqueur and marmalade, then fold into the cream until evenly distributed.

HOT CHOCOLATE SOUFFLÉ

| 1.00 | £ £ | 629 cals |

Serves 4

50 g (2 oz) caster sugar, plus extra to coat

50 g (2 oz) plain chocolate, broken into pieces

45 ml (3 tbsp) brandy

25 g (1 oz) butter or margarine

15 g ($\frac{1}{2}$ oz) plain flour

150 ml ($\frac{1}{4}$ pint) milk

3 egg yolks and 4 egg whites

icing sugar, to dredge

hot chocolate sauce (see page 156), to serve

5 Whisk the egg whites until stiff, then fold into the chocolate mixture. Turn into the prepared soufflé dish and bake immediately in the oven at 200°C (400°F) mark 6 for 35 minutes until well risen. Dredge with icing sugar and serve the soufflé immediately, with hot chocolate sauce handed separately.

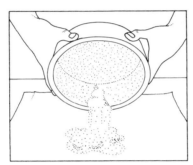

1 Coat the inside of a greased 15-cm (6-inch) soufflé dish with caster sugar. Shake off the excess sugar.

2 Put the chocolate and brandy in a heatproof bowl standing over a pan of simmering water. Heat gently until melted. Remove bowl from the pan.

3 Melt the fat in a separate saucepan, add the flour and cook for 2 minutes, stirring all the time. Remove from the heat and gradually add the milk, then return to the heat and bring to the boil, stirring. Simmer for 2 minutes until thick and smooth.

4 Remove the pan from the heat and stir in the caster sugar, melted chocolate and egg yolks, one at a time.

TIPS ON MAKING A HOT SOUFFLÉ

Making a hot soufflé is easier than you think. Here are a few helpful hints for success every time:

● Preheat the oven to the required temperature before starting the recipe, and preheat a baking sheet on the centre shelf at the same time. This ensures that the soufflé starts cooking immediately it is put into the oven. Remove any shelves above the centre shelf before baking to allow room for rising.

● Make sure the egg whites are whisked stiffly before folding them into the sauce mixture. To test if they are stiff enough, turn the bowl upside down — they should not drop.

● To lighten the sauce mixture, fold a tablespoon of the stiffly whisked egg whites into the sauce before folding in the rest.

MARBLED APRICOT SOUFFLÉ

2.00* 🕮 £ £ ✱

439–585 cals

* plus overnight soaking, 1½ hours cooling and 4 hours setting

Serves 6–8

225 g (8 oz) dried apricots, soaked overnight in cold water

180 ml (12 tbsp) water

175 g (6 oz) caster sugar

30 ml (2 tbsp) almond-flavoured liqueur

15 ml (3 tsp) gelatine

4 eggs, separated

300 ml (10 fl oz) double cream

few drops of orange food colouring

ratafia biscuits and whipped cream, to decorate

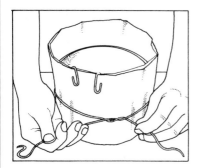

1 Prepare a 15-cm (6-inch) soufflé dish: cut a double thickness of greaseproof paper long enough to go around the outside of the dish and 5–7.5 cm (2–3 inches) deeper. Secure the dish around the outside with paper clips and string.

2 Drain the soaked dried apricots, then put them in a saucepan with 120 ml (8 tbsp) of the water and 50 g (2 oz) of the sugar. Heat gently until the sugar has dissolved, then cover and simmer for about 30 minutes until tender. Leave to cool slightly, then rub through a sieve or purée in a blender. Stir in the liqueur and leave to cool for about 30 minutes.

3 Meanwhile, place the remaining water in a small heatproof bowl and sprinkle in the gelatine. Stand the bowl over a saucepan of hot water and heat gently until dissolved. Remove the bowl from the water and cool slightly.

4 Put the egg yolks and remaining sugar in a large heatproof bowl and stand over the pan of gently simmering water. Whisk until the mixture is thick and holds a ribbon trail, then remove from the heat and leave for about 1 hour until cold, whisking occasionally.

5 Whip the cream until it will stand in soft peaks. Whisk the egg whites until stiff.

6 Stir the gelatine liquid into the apricot purée, then fold this into the egg yolk mixture until evenly blended. Next fold in the whipped cream, then egg whites.

7 Transfer half the mixture to a separate bowl and tint with the food colouring.

8 Put alternate spoonfuls of the two mixtures into the prepared soufflé dish. Level the surface, then chill in the refrigerator for at least 4 hours until set.

9 Carefully remove the paper from the edge of the soufflé. Press the crushed ratafias around the exposed edge. Decorate top with apricots and whipped cream.

MERINGUE SURPRISE CASSIS

0.45*	▯ ▯ £ £ ✳

370–493 cals

* plus 1 hour cooling and at least
4 hours freezing

Serves 6–8

15 ml (1 tbsp) arrowroot
6 egg yolks and 2 egg whites
50 g (2 oz) vanilla sugar
300 ml (½ pint) milk
300 ml (10 fl oz) double cream
16 baby meringues
350 g (12 oz) frozen blackcurrants
juice of 1 lemon
50 g (2 oz) icing sugar, or to taste
45 ml (3 tbsp) blackcurrant liqueur

1 Put the arrowroot in a heat-proof bowl and blend to a paste with the egg yolks and vanilla sugar.

2 Scald the milk by bringing it up to boiling point, then stir slowly into the egg yolk mixture.

3 Stand the bowl over a pan of gently simmering water and stir until the custard is thick enough to coat the back of a wooden spoon.

4 Remove from the heat, cover the surface of the custard closely with cling film to prevent a skin forming and leave for 1 hour.

5 Whip the cream until it just holds its shape, then fold into the cold custard. Whisk the egg whites until stiff, then fold in until evenly incorporated.

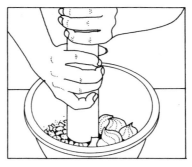

6 Crush 10 of the meringues roughly and fold into the custard mixture until evenly distributed.

7 Base-line an 18-cm (6-inch) Charlotte mould, soufflé dish or cake tin with non-stick parchment paper. Pour in the custard mixture, cover the mould, then freeze for at least 4 hours or overnight until solid.

8 Meanwhile, make the blackcurrant sauce. Reserve a few whole frozen blackcurrants for decoration.

9 Put the remaining frozen blackcurrants and the lemon juice in a heavy-based saucepan and heat gently until defrosted, shaking the pan constantly.

10 Cook gently for 10 minutes, then tip into a sieve and press with the back of a spoon to extract as much juice as possible.

11 Sift the icing sugar into the blackcurrant juice, then stir in the liqueur. Leave until cold, taste and add more sugar if liked.

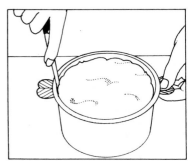

12 To serve, run a knife around the dessert in the mould, then carefully turn out on to a serving plate. Remove paper.

13 Pour a little of the sauce over the dessert, then decorate with the reserved blackcurrants and the remaining meringues. Serve at once, with the remaining sauce handed separately.

—— VARIATION ——

Although frozen blackcurrants are available at most large supermarkets and freezer centres, raspberries are more readily available, and can equally well be used for this recipe. Replace the blackcurrant liqueur with *framboise*, a French raspberry liqueur sold in good off-licences. Alternatively, kirsch (a liqueur made from cherries which is available in miniature bottles), goes well with the flavour of raspberries—and blackcurrants too.

BANANA CHARTREUSE

4.00* ⬜ £ £ 290–435 cals

* plus 1½ hours cooling

Serves 4–6

135-g (4¾-oz) packet lemon jelly,
    broken into squares
300 ml (½ pint) boiling water
3 bananas
juice of ½ a lemon
about 6 shelled pistachio nuts
15 ml (3 tsp) gelatine
60 ml (4 tbsp) dark rum
150 ml (5 fl oz) double cream
50 g (2 oz) icing sugar, sifted

1 Make up the jelly according to the packet instructions, using only 300 ml (½ pint) boiling water. Cool for 30 minutes.

2 Pour about one third of the jelly into a chilled 18-cm (6-inch) charlotte mould. Chill for 30 minutes until set.

3 Peel 1 banana, slice thinly, then sprinkle with a little lemon juice to prevent browning.

4 Arrange the banana slices on top of the set jelly in an attractive pattern. Cut the pistachios in half lengthways and place between or around the banana slices.

5 Slowly spoon over the remaining cool jelly, taking care not to dislodge the pattern of bananas and pistachios. Chill for 30 minutes until set.

6 Sprinkle the gelatine over the rum and remaining lemon juice in a small heatproof bowl. Stand the bowl over a saucepan of hot water and heat gently until dissolved. Cool for 5 minutes.

7 Whip the cream with the icing sugar. Peel and mash the remaining bananas, then combine with the cream and cooled gelatine liquid. Spoon on top of the set jelly and chill in the refrigerator for about 2 hours until set.

8 To serve, dip base of mould in hot water for a few seconds, then invert banana chartreuse on to a serving plate. Serve chilled.

CHARTREUSE

The word *chartreuse* in French culinary terms can mean several different things. It is the name of a yellow or green liqueur made by the monks at the abbey of Chartreuse. *En chartreuse* is a term used to describe a game bird which is stewed with cabbage. Or, as here, it can be used to describe a dessert made with jelly.

RASPBERRY WALNUT TORTE

| 1.45* | 🔲 | £ £ | 539 cals |

* plus 30 minutes chilling

Serves 8

100 g (4 oz) walnuts

100 g (4 oz) unsalted butter

75 g (3 oz) caster sugar

175 g (6 oz) plain flour

450 g (1 lb) fresh raspberries

50 g (2 oz) icing sugar

30 ml (2 tbsp) raspberry-flavoured liqueur or kirsch (optional)

300 ml (10 fl oz) double cream

150 ml (5 fl oz) single cream

1 Grind the walnuts finely in a mouli grater, electric blender or food processor.

2 Cream the butter and sugar together until light and fluffy, then beat in the walnuts and flour. Divide the dough into three.

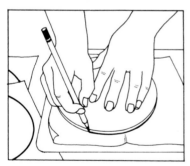

3 Draw three 20.5-cm (8-inch) circles on non-stick baking parchment. Place these on baking sheets.

4 Put a piece of dough in the centre of each circle and press with the heel of your hand until dough is same size as circle.

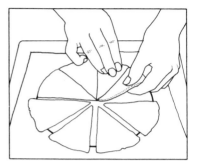

5 Cut one of the circles into eight triangles with a sharp knife and ease them slightly apart. Refrigerate the pastries for 30 minutes. Bake in the oven at

190°C (375°F) mark 5 for 15–20 minutes, swapping over the sheets to ensure the pastries brown evenly. Leave to cool and harden for 10 minutes on the paper, then transfer to wire racks to cool completely.

6 Meanwhile, reserve one third of the whole raspberries for decoration. Put the rest in a bowl with the icing sugar and liqueur, if using. Crush the fruit with a fork, then leave to macerate while the pastry is cooling.

7 Assemble the torte just before serving. Whip the creams together until thick, then fold in the crushed raspberries and juice. Stand one round of pastry on a flat serving plate and spread with half of the cream mixture. Top with the remaining round of pastry and the remaining cream mixture.

8 Arrange the triangles of pastry on top of the cream, wedging them in at an angle. Scatter the reserved whole raspberries in between. Serve as soon as possible.

NON-STICK BAKING PARCHMENT

The pastry for this torte is made with ground walnuts, which make it oily and therefore more prone to sticking than ordinary pastries. Whereas greaseproof paper and foil can be used for most baking, non-stick baking parchment is recommended here because it is silicone treated and by far the best paper to use for sticky or oily mixtures. Buy it by the roll at large supermarkets, hardware stores and specialist kitchen shops.

MERINGUE BASKET

6.00* ⬚ ⬚ £ 317–423 cals

* plus 20 minutes cooling
Serves 6–8

4 egg whites
225 g (8 oz) icing sugar
1 small pineapple
3 bananas
300 ml (10 fl oz) whipping cream
30 ml (2 tbsp) kirsch
coarsely grated chocolate,
**   to decorate**

1 Line three baking sheets with non-stick baking parchment (turn rimmed baking sheets upside down and use the bases), and draw a 19-cm (7½-inch) circle on each. Turn the paper over so that the pencilled circle is visible but does not come into contact with the meringues and mark them.

2 Place 3 egg whites in a clean, dry heatproof bowl, and place the bowl over a pan of simmering water. Sift in 175 g (6 oz) of the icing sugar.

3 Whisk the egg whites and sugar vigorously over the simmering water until the mixture stands in very stiff peaks. Do not allow the bowl to get too hot or the meringue will crust around edges.

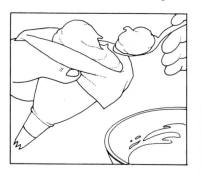

4 Fit a piping bag with a large star nozzle. Spoon in one third of the meringue mixture. Secure the paper to the baking sheets with a little meringue.

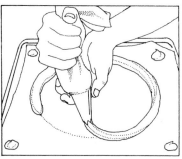

5 Pipe rings of meringue about 1 cm (½ inch) thick inside two of the circles on the paper.

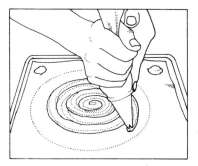

6 Fill the bag with the remaining meringue and, starting from centre, pipe a continuous coil of meringue on the third sheet of paper. Place all in the oven at 100°C (200°F) gas mark Low for 2½–3 hours to dry out.

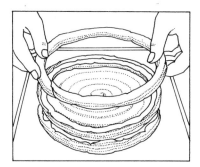

7 Use the remaining egg white and sugar to make meringue as before and put into the piping bag. Remove the cooked meringue rings from the paper and layer up on the base, piping a ring of fresh meringue between each. Return to oven for a further 1½–2 hours. Slide on to a wire rack and peel off base paper when cool.

8 Cut the pineapple across into 1-cm (½-inch) slices and snip off skin. Cut out core and divide flesh into bite-size chunks. Peel bananas and cut into 1-cm (½-inch) slices. Mix the fruits together, reserving a little pineapple and banana for decoration.

9 Just before serving, stand the meringue shell on a flat serving plate. Lightly whip the cream and fold in the kirsch; spoon half into the base of the basket and top with the fruit. Whirl the remaining cream over the top and decorate with the reserved pineapple, banana and the grated chocolate.

MAKING MERINGUES

There are three basic types of meringue. *Meringue suisse* is the most common and the most simple—egg whites are stiffly whisked, then caster sugar is folded in. *Meringue cuite* is the type of meringue used for this basket. It is firmer than *meringue suisse* and therefore better able to hold up when filled with fruit and cream as here. Although its name suggests that it is cooked, it is in fact only whisked over hot water before being baked in the same way as *meringue suisse*. *Meringue italienne* is made by combining sugar syrup with egg whites; it is difficult to make, and mostly used by professionals.

Traditional and Everyday Desserts

Here you will find the family favourites which everyone enjoys whenever you make them, but which tend to get forgotten when there are so many new things to try. Traditional pies, tarts and crumbles are here, plus the more old-fashioned trifles, cobblers and crowdies. Serve them for everyday puds, or at a dinner party. You'll be surprised how much your family and friends will welcome a delicious reminder of the past.

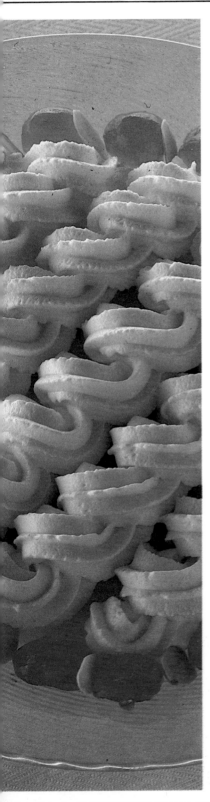

OLD ENGLISH TRIFLE

1.00* ☐ £ £ 604 cals

* plus 30 minutes cooling and 12 hours chilling

Serves 6

568 ml (1 pint) milk
½ vanilla pod
2 eggs
2 egg yolks
30 ml (2 tbsp) caster sugar, plus extra for sprinkling
8 trifle sponges
100 g (4 oz) apricot jam
100 g (4 oz) macaroons, lightly crushed
100 ml (4 fl oz) medium sherry
300 ml (10 fl oz) whipping cream
50 g (2 oz) glacé cherries, halved
40 g (1½ oz) flaked almonds, toasted

1 Heat the milk with the vanilla pod until it reaches boiling point. Remove from the heat, cover and leave to infuse for about 20 minutes.

2 Beat together the eggs, egg yolks and 30 ml (2 tbsp) sugar. Strain milk on to the mixture. Return to pan and cook over gentle heat for about 10 minutes without boiling, stirring all the time until the custard thickens slightly.

3 Pour the custard into a bowl, lightly sprinkle the surface with sugar, then leave to cool for 30 minutes.

4 Slice the trifle sponges in half and sandwich together with jam, cut up and place in a 2-litre (3½-pint) shallow serving dish with the macaroons. Spoon over the sherry, then pour over the cold custard. Cover and refrigerate for about 12 hours.

5 Whip the cream until stiff. Top the custard with half the cream and pipe the remaining cream on top. Decorate the trifle with cherries and flaked almonds before serving.

MAKING EGG CUSTARD

Egg custard is traditional in an English trifle, but curdling can be a problem. Use a heavy-bottomed pan (cast iron is best) and keep the heat very gentle until the mixture thickens. Don't be impatient to hurry the thickening along by increasing the heat—this will almost certainly result in a lumpy or grainy custard. A useful tip is to combine the eggs and sugar with 5 ml (1 tsp) cornflour before adding the milk. Cornflour helps stabilise the mixture, but it does not taste in the finished trifle.

LIME MERINGUE PIE

1.35*	f	520 cals

* plus 30 minutes chilling

Serves 6

200 g (7 oz) shortcrust pastry (see page 155)

2 limes

75 g (3 oz) granulated sugar

45 ml (3 tbsp) cornflour

2 eggs, separated

knob of butter

125 g (4 oz) caster sugar

lime slices, to decorate (optional)

pouring cream, to serve

1 Roll out the pastry on a floured work surface and use to line a 20.5-cm (8-inch) flan ring. Refrigerate for 30 minutes. Bake blind in the oven at 200°C (400°F) mark 6 for 10–15 minutes.

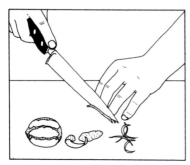

2 Pare a few strips of lime peel, shred finely, blanch in boiling water for 1 minute, drain, cool.

3 Finely grate the remaining rind from the limes into a small saucepan. Strain the juice, make up to 300 ml ($\frac{1}{2}$ pint) with water and add to the pan with the granulated sugar. Heat gently to dissolve the sugar.

4 Blend the cornflour with 30 ml (2 tbsp) water to a smooth paste. Add some of the heated liquid and stir. Return to the pan and boil for 2 minutes, stirring all the time. Cool slightly, then beat in the egg yolks and butter. Pour into the warm pastry case.

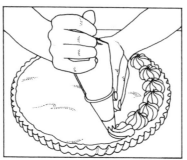

5 Whisk the egg whites until stiff, then fold in the caster sugar. Spread a thin layer of meringue over the pie, then pipe the rest around the edge.

6 Bake in the oven at 150°C (300°F) mark 2 for about 45 minutes until the meringue is crisp and lightly browned.

7 Decorate with the shredded lime rind and slices (if using). Serve the pie warm, with cream.

BAKEWELL PUDDING

0.45	£	659–933 cals

Serves 4–6

225 g (8 oz) frozen puff pastry, thawed, or shortcrust pastry (see page 155)

45 ml (3 tbsp) red jam

175 g (6 oz) ground almonds

100 g (4 oz) caster sugar

50 g (2 oz) unsalted butter

3 eggs, beaten

1.25 ml ($\frac{1}{4}$ tsp) almond flavouring

pouring cream or custard, to serve

1 Roll out the pastry on a floured surface and use to line a 900-ml (1$\frac{1}{2}$-pint) oval pie dish.

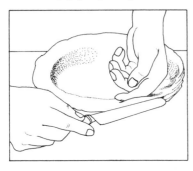

2 Knock up the edge of the pastry in the pie dish with the back of a knife.

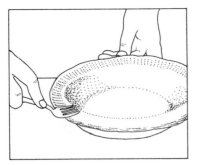

3 Mark the rim with the prongs of a fork. Brush the jam over the base. Chill in the refrigerator while making the filling.

4 Make the filling. Beat the almonds with the sugar, butter, eggs and almond flavouring.

5 Pour the filling over the jam and spread it evenly. Bake in the oven at 200°C (400°F) mark 6 for 30 minutes or until the filling is set. Serve warm or cold, with pouring cream or custard.

BAKEWELL PUDDING
This rich pudding was first created by the cook at an inn in Bakewell, Derbyshire in 1859. It is still made in the town today, according to a secret recipe. Our version is like the original, and not to be confused with the similar but drier Bakewell tart, which is made with bread or cake crumbs.

OLD-FASHIONED TREACLE TART

1.00 £ 528–721 cals

Serves 4–6

150 g (6 oz) plain flour

pinch of salt

40 g (1½ oz) caster sugar

50 g (2 oz) butter or block margarine

25 g (1 oz) lard

15–30 ml (1–2 tbsp) iced water

225 g (8 oz) golden syrup

finely grated rind and juice of 1 lemon

75 g (3 oz) fresh white breadcrumbs

a little beaten egg or milk, to glaze

whipped cream, to serve

1 Place the flour and salt into a bowl, then stir in the sugar. Rub in half the butter or margarine with the lard until the mixture resembles fine bread-crumbs. Add enough iced water to mix to a firm dough.

2 Gather the dough together with your fingers and form into a ball, then roll out on a floured surface and use to line a 20.5-cm (8-inch) loose-bottomed flan tin. Reserve the pastry trim-mings. Chill in the refrigerator while making the filling.

3 Make the filling. Warm the golden syrup in a heavy-based pan with the remaining butter and the lemon rind and juice.

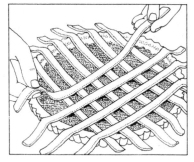

4 Sprinkle the breadcrumbs evenly over the base of the pastry case, then slowly pour in the melted syrup.

5 Make strips from the reserved pastry trimmings and place these over the tart in a lattice pattern, brushing the ends with water to stick them to the pastry case. Glaze with a little beaten egg or milk.

6 Bake in the oven at 190°C (375°F) mark 5 for about 25 minutes until the filling is just set. Serve warm, with whipped cream.

TREACLE

You may wonder why recipes for treacle tart always contain golden syrup rather than treacle. The explanation is quite simple. Treacle is the syrup which is left in the sugar refining process when the sugar has been crystal-lised; in the seventeenth century, when West Indian sugar cane was first refined to make sugar, treacle was unrefined and recipes

for treacle tart such as this one would have used black treacle rather than syrup. It was not until the late nineteenth century that treacle itself was refined to make the golden syrup which is so popular today. As tastes changed, recipes which had originally used treacle began to specify syrup instead.

COLLEGE PUDDINGS

| 0.50 | £ | 473 cals |

Serves 4

100 g (4 oz) shredded suet

100 g (4 oz) fresh white breadcrumbs

50 g (2 oz) sultanas

50 g (2 oz) raisins

pinch of ground cinnamon

pinch of ground cloves

pinch of grated nutmeg

50 g (2 oz) sugar

2.5 ml ($\frac{1}{2}$ tsp) baking powder

pinch of salt

2 eggs, beaten

custard sauce, to serve (see page 149)

1 Mix the suet with the breadcrumbs and add the fruit, spices, sugar, baking powder and salt. Mix very well together, then stir in the eggs.

2 Pour into four greased dariole moulds or small individual foil dishes placed on a baking tray and bake in the oven at 180°C (350°F) mark 4 for about 30 minutes. Turn out and serve hot with custard.

SPICED APPLE AND PLUM CRUMBLE

1.10* £ ✳	402 cals

*plus 30 minutes cooling

Serves 6

450 g (1 lb) plums

700 g (1½ lb) cooking apples

100 g (4 oz) butter or margarine

100 g (4 oz) sugar

7.5 ml (1½ tsp) ground mixed spice

175 g (6 oz) plain wholewheat flour

50 g (2 oz) blanched hazelnuts, toasted and chopped

1 Using a sharp knife, cut the plums in half and then carefully remove the stones.

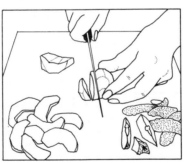

2 Peel, quarter, core and slice the apples. Place in a medium saucepan with 25 g (1 oz) fat, half the sugar and about 5 ml (1 tsp) mixed spice.

3 Cover the pan and cook gently for 15 minutes until the apples begin to soften. Stir in the plums and turn into a 1.1-litre (2-pint) shallow ovenproof dish. Leave to cool for about 30 minutes.

4 Stir the flour and remaining mixed spice well together, then rub in the remaining fat until the mixture resembles fine breadcrumbs. Stir in the rest of the sugar with the chopped hazelnuts.

5 Spoon the crumble mixture over the fruit and bake in the oven at 180°C (350°F) mark 4 for about 40 minutes or until the top is golden, crisp and crumbly.

PLUMS FOR COOKING

All plums can be cooked, but dessert varieties tend to be more expensive, therefore it makes good sense to look for cooking plums. Unfortunately, green-grocers and supermarkets do not always specify the variety of plums on sale, but it is always worth asking. Whether you cook with red or yellow plums is entirely a matter of personal choice, but cooking plums worth looking for are Czars, small red cherry plums, Pershore Yellow Egg, Purple Pershore and Belle de Loutain. The famous Victoria plum is a dual purpose fruit: sweet and juicy, it is equally suitable for cooking and eating. Greengages and damsons come from the same family as the plum, and can be used in any recipe calling for plums, although extra sugar may be required.

AMERICAN CHOCOLATE PIE

| 1.00* | 🍴 | £ | 609 cals |

* plus 30 minutes chilling and 4 hours setting

Serves 8

225 g (8 oz) shortcrust pastry (see page 155

100 g (4 oz) sugar

50 g (2 oz) plain flour

pinch of salt

450 ml ($\frac{3}{4}$ pint) milk

50 g (2 oz) plain chocolate

3 egg yolks

40 g ($1\frac{1}{2}$ oz) butter or margarine

5 ml (1 tsp) vanilla flavouring

225 ml (8 fl oz) double or whipping cream

chocolate curls (see page 147) or grated chocolate, to decorate

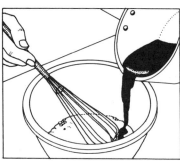

1 Roll out the pastry on a lightly floured surface and use to line a 23-cm (9-inch) loose-bottomed fluted flan tin or ring placed on a baking sheet. Crimp edges of pastry and refrigerate for 30 minutes.

2 Prick the base of the pastry case then bake blind in the oven at 200°C (400°F) mark 6 for 10–15 minutes until set. Remove paper and beans and bake for a further 5–10 minutes until lightly coloured. Leave to cool.

3 While the pastry case is cooling, mix the sugar with the flour and salt in a large saucepan and stir in the milk.

4 Break the chocolate into small pieces and add to the pan. Heat gently until the chocolate has melted, stirring continuously.

5 Whisk until the chocolate and milk are blended, then increase the heat and cook for about 10 minutes, stirring constantly. Remove saucepan from heat.

6 Beat the egg yolks and whisk in a small amount of the hot chocolate sauce.

7 Slowly pour the egg mixture into the saucepan, stirring rapidly. Cook over low heat stirring, for 10–15 minutes, until the mixture is very thick and creamy. Do not allow to boil.

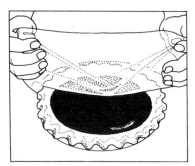

8 Remove from the heat. Stir in the fat and vanilla flavouring and pour into the cold pastry case. Cover to prevent a skin forming and refrigerate for about 4 hours until set.

9 Just before serving, whip the cream lightly and spread it evenly over the chocolate filling. Decorate the top with chocolate curls or grated chocolate. Serve the pie chilled.

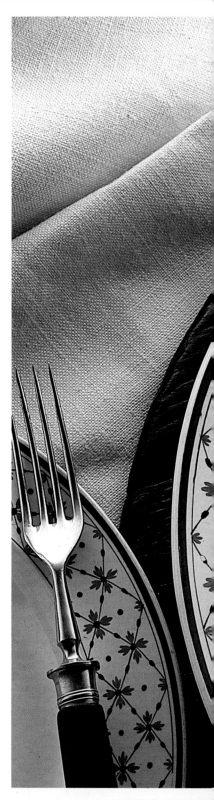

BLACKBERRY AND PEAR COBBLER

| 0.45 | £ | ✳ | 424 cals |

Serves 4

450 g (1 lb) blackberries

450 g (1 lb) ripe cooking pears (e.g. Conference)

finely grated rind and juice of 1 lemon

2.5 ml ($\frac{1}{2}$ tsp) ground cinnamon

225 g (8 oz) self raising flour

pinch of salt

50 g (2 oz) butter or block margarine

25 g (1 oz) caster sugar

about 150 ml ($\frac{1}{4}$ pint) milk plus extra to glaze

1 Pick over the blackberries and wash them. Peel and core the pears, then slice them thickly.

2 Put the blackberries and pears into a saucepan with the lemon rind and juice and the cinnamon. Poach gently for 15 or 20 minutes until the fruit is juicy and tender.

3 Meanwhile, place the flour and salt into the bowl. Rub in the fat, then stir in the sugar. Gradually add the milk to mix to a fairly soft dough.

4 Roll out the dough on a floured work surface until 1.5 cm ($\frac{1}{2}$ inch) thick. Cut out rounds using a fluted 5-cm (2-inch) pastry cutter.

5 Put the fruit in a pie dish and top with overlapping pastry rounds, leaving a gap in the centre. Brush the top of the pastry rounds with milk. Bake in the oven at 220°C (425°F) mark 7 for 10–15 minutes until pastry is golden brown. Serve hot.

COBBLER

Recipes with the strange-sounding title of 'cobbler' are invariably American in origin, although very little is known for certain about the meaning behind the word in culinary terms. Cobblers can be sweet or savoury; they always have a scone dough topping which is stamped into small rounds — sometimes the whole surface of the dish is covered with these rounds of dough, although often they are simply placed around the outside to reveal the filling in the centre. One theory is that the word cobbler originates from the fact that the rounds of dough look like 'cobbles' or stones.

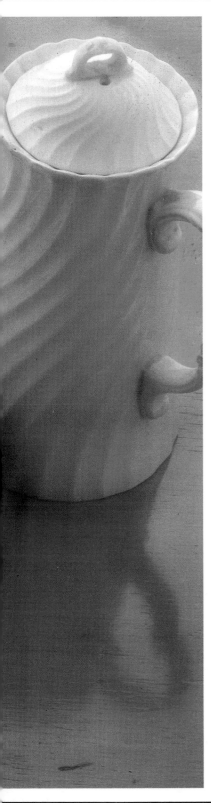

ALMOND EVE'S PUDDING

1.30	£	784 cals

Serves 4

700 g (1½ lb) cooking apples
5 ml (1 tsp) ground cinnamon
175 g (6 oz) demerara sugar
125 g (4 oz) butter, softened
2 eggs, beaten
125 g (4 oz) self raising flour
25 g (1 oz) ground almonds
2.5 ml (½ tsp) almond flavouring
30 ml (2 tbsp) milk
25 g (1 oz) flaked almonds
icing sugar, to dredge
single cream, to serve

1 Peel, quarter and core the cooking apples, then slice them thickly into a 1.4-litre (2½-pint) ovenproof dish. Combine the cinnamon with 50 g (2 oz) of the demerara sugar and scatter over the apples. Cover tightly with cling film while preparing the topping.

2 Beat the butter and remaining sugar, creaming them together until fluffy. Gradually beat in eggs.

3 Fold in the flour, ground almonds, flavouring and milk. Spread the mixture over the cooking apples.

4 Place the flaked almonds on top in six squares to form a chequerboard effect. Bake in the oven at 180°C (350°F) mark 4 for 50–60 minutes until the apples are tender and the sponge risen and golden brown.

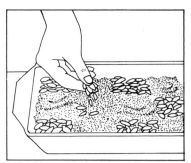

5 Dredge icing sugar between the flaked nut squares. Serve with cream.

------ VARIATION ------

If liked, you can add 50 g (2 oz) sultanas, currants or raisins to the apple mixture in the base of this delicious family pudding. Grated orange or lemon zest added to the sponge topping also adds extra flavour—and goes particularly well with the cinnamon-flavoured apples.

LOCKSHEN PUDDING

| 1.00 | £ | 356 cals |

Serves 4

100 g (4 oz) vermicelli (lockshen)

pinch of salt

1 egg

50 g (2 oz) sugar

1.25 ml ($\frac{1}{4}$ tsp) ground cinnamon

finely grated rind of $\frac{1}{2}$ a lemon

50 g (2 oz) currants

50 g (2 oz) chopped almonds
 (optional)

25 g (1 oz) margarine

1 Drop the vermicelli into rapidly boiling salted water and cook for about 10 minutes until tender.

2 Drain into a sieve and rinse with plenty of hot water to remove excess starch. Drain well.

3 Whisk the egg and sugar together and stir in the cinnamon, rind, currants and nuts, if using. Then stir in the vermicelli.

4 Melt the margarine in a 5-cm (2-inch) deep, flameproof baking dish until hot but not smoking. Swirl around the dish to coat the sides and pour the excess into the noodle mixture.

5 Stir well and pour the mixture into the baking dish. Bake in the oven at 190°C (375°F) mark 5 for 45 minutes until set, crisp and brown on top. Serve hot.

CREAM CROWDIE

0.30*	£	481 cals

* plus 1 hour refrigeration and 30 minutes standing time

Serves 4

50 g (2 oz) medium oatmeal

300 ml (10 fl oz) double cream

60 ml (4 tbsp) clear honey

45 ml (3 tbsp) whisky

350 g (12 oz) fresh raspberries, hulled

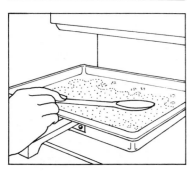

1 Place the oatmeal in a grill pan (without the rack) and toast until golden brown, turning occasionally with a spoon. Leave for 15 minutes until cool.

2 Whip the cream until just standing in soft peaks, then stir in the honey, whisky and cooled toasted oatmeal.

3 Reserve a few raspberries for decoration, then layer up the remaining raspberries and fresh cream mixture in four tall glasses. Cover with cling film and refrigerate for at least 1 hour.

4 Allow to come to room temperature for 30 minutes before serving. Decorate each glass with the reserved raspberries.

CROWDIE

In Scotland, *crowdie* can mean a cream cheese or a kind of porridge. This recipe for cream crowdie is so called because it contains oatmeal, which the Scots use for making porridge.

YORKSHIRE CURD TART

1.00	£	✳	290–435 cals

Makes 8–12 slices

225 g (8 oz) plain flour
pinch of salt
125 g (5 oz) butter or block margarine
1 egg yolk
about 30 ml (2 tbsp) cold water
450 g (1 lb) curd cheese
3 eggs, beaten
75 g (3 oz) currants
100 g (4 oz) demerara sugar
finely grated rind of 1 lemon

1 Make the pastry: place the flour and salt into a bowl, add 100 g (4 oz) of the fat and rub in until the mixture resembles fine breadcrumbs. Stir in the egg yolk, and enough water to bind the mixture together. Form into a ball.

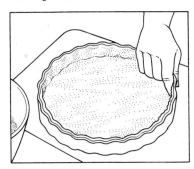

2 Roll out the pastry on a floured work surface. Use to line a 20.5-cm (8½-inch) fluted flan dish or sandwich tin, then refrigerate while making the curd cheese filling.

3 Put the curd cheese in a bowl and stir in the eggs, followed by the currants, sugar and lemon rind. Melt the remaining fat and stir in until evenly mixed.

4 Pour the filling into the pastry case, place on a preheated baking sheet and bake in the oven at 190°C (375°F) mark 5 for 45 minutes or until the filling is golden and set. Serve the tart warm or cold.

CURDS

This recipe for Yorkshire curd tart used curd cheese, but in Yorkshire it is traditional to use homemade curds. These are made by adding Epsom salts and lemon juice to fresh milk, which then becomes curdled when left overnight. The whey is strained off and the curds are used in cooking.

DANISH 'PEASANT GIRL IN A VEIL'

| 0.30* | £ | 601 cals |

* plus cooling and 2–3 hours chilling

Serves 4

50 g (2 oz) butter or margarine

175 g (6 oz) fresh breadcrumbs

75 g (3 oz) soft brown sugar

700 g (1½ lb) cooking apples

30 ml (2 tbsp) water

juice of ½ a lemon

sugar to taste

150 ml (5 fl oz) double or whipping cream

50 g (2 oz) grated chocolate, to decorate

1 Melt the fat in a frying pan. Mix the crumbs and sugar together and fry in the hot fat until crisp, stirring frequently with a wooden spoon to prevent the crumbs from catching and burning.

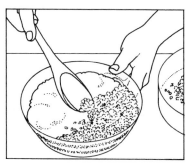

2 Peel, core and slice the apples. Put them in a saucepan with the water, lemon juice and some sugar to taste. Cover and cook gently for 10–15 minutes until they form a pulp. Leave to cool, then taste for sweetness.

3 Put alternate layers of the fried crumb mixture and the apple pulp into a glass dish, finishing with a layer of crumbs. Refrigerate for 2–3 hours.

4 Whip the cream until stiff. Pipe over the top of the crumb mixture and decorate with grated chocolate. Serve chilled.

DANISH 'PEASANT GIRL IN A VEIL'

This simple but delicious pudding of stewed apples layered with fried breadcrumbs and sugar is very similar to an apple charlotte. In Denmark, where it is called _bondepige med slør_, it takes its name from the fact that the apple and crumbs are 'veiled' or covered with cream. Like apple charlotte, it is a country-style pudding, yet it tastes so good that it would be perfect for any type of special occasion,

especially if made in a glass bowl so that the layers can be seen.

You can ring the changes by using different breadcrumbs. White breadcrumbs can of course be used, but wholemeal or granary bread give a more nutty texture. In Denmark, rye bread would be used to make the crumbs, so if you can find a bakery or Jewish delicatessen that sells rye bread, it is well worth trying.

MAGIC CHOCOLATE PUDDING

| 0.45 | £ | 241–362 cals |

Serves 4–6

50 g (2 oz) butter or margarine

75 g (3 oz) caster sugar

2 eggs, separated

40 g (1½ oz) self raising flour

25 ml (5 tsp) cocoa powder

350 ml (12 fl oz) milk

1 Cream the fat and sugar together until light and fluffy, then beat in the egg yolks.

2 Sift the flour and cocoa powder together over the creamed mixture, then beat in until evenly mixed. Stir in the milk. Whisk the egg whites until stiff and fold into the mixture.

3 Pour into a greased 1-litre (1¾-pint) ovenproof dish. Bake in the oven at 180°C (350°F) mark 4 for 35–45 minutes until the top is set and spongy to the touch. This pudding will separate into a custard layer with a sponge topping. Serve hot.

MAGIC CHOCOLATE PUDDING

This delicious chocolate pudding, which is a great hit with children, is called 'magic' because it separates magically during baking into a rich chocolate sauce at the bottom and a sponge cake on top.

CHRISTMAS PUDDING

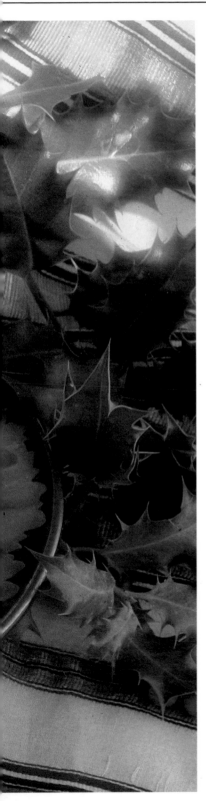

| 0.20* £ £ | 611–736 cals |

* plus overnight maturing, 8 hours steaming, 2 hours cooling, 1 month maturing and 3 hours reheating

Serves 8–10

| 50 g (2 oz) dried figs |
| 50 g (2 oz) stoned prunes |
| 50 g (2 oz) dried dates |
| 50 g (2 oz) glacé cherries |
| 125 g (4 oz) sultanas |
| 125 g (4 oz) currants |
| 125 g (4 oz) raisins |
| 50 g (2 oz) cut mixed peel |
| 150 g (5 oz) plain flour |
| 150 g (5 oz) dark soft brown sugar |
| 125 g (4 oz) fresh brown breadcrumbs |
| 225 g (8 oz) shredded suet |
| 5 ml (1 tsp) ground mixed spice |
| 5 ml (1 tsp) salt |
| 2.5 ml ($\frac{1}{2}$ tsp) grated nutmeg |
| 3 eggs |
| 75 ml (5 tbsp) milk |
| 250 ml (8 fl oz) stout |
| 10 ml (2 tsp) lemon juice |
| pouring custard, to serve |

1 Roughly chop the figs, prune flesh, dates and cherries. Then, in a large bowl, mix all the dry ingredients together.

2 Whisk together the eggs, milk, stout and lemon juice. Stir into the dry ingredients, mixing well. Cover and leave to cool overnight.

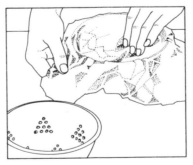

3 Line the two halves of a rice-steaming ball with foil so that it protrudes beyond the rim of each half. Fill with the mixture.

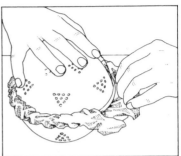

4 Close up the lined rice-steaming ball and twist the protruding foil edges together.

5 Cook in a pan of rapidly boiling water for at least 8 hours, topping up the water as necessary.

6 When cooked, remove pudding from the pan and leave to cool for at least 2 hours. Remove from the steaming ball, unwrap foil then rewrap in greaseproof paper and fresh foil.

7 Store in a cool place to mature for at least 1 month. To serve, place the pudding in a pan of rapidly boiling water and boil for at least 3 hours. Serve with custard.

CHRISTMAS PUDDINGS

Round Christmas puddings like this one were traditional in Victorian and Edwardian times, but with the popularity of the china pudding basin, they seemed to go out of fashion. Your family and friends will really appreciate your reviving an old custom at Christmas time, so it is well worth investing in a rice-steaming ball—it can be used all year round for other steamed puddings as well as for cooking rice. Look for rice-steaming balls in specialist kitchen shops, where you may also find special round metal Christmas pudding moulds, which seem to be coming back into fashion again.

SUSSEX POND PUDDING

| 4.30 | 🍶 | f | 649 cals |

Serves 6

| 350 g (12 oz) self raising flour |
| 2.5 ml ($\frac{1}{2}$ tsp) salt |
| 175 g (6 oz) shredded suet |
| about 175 ml (6 fl oz) water |
| 100 g (4 oz) butter, cut into pieces |
| 100 g (4 oz) demerara sugar |
| 1 large lemon |

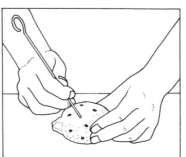

1 Place the flour and salt into a bowl, then stir in the suet and enough cold water to make a light, elastic dough. Knead lightly until it is smooth.

2 Roll out two thirds of the pastry on a floured work surface to a circle, 2.5 cm (1 inch) larger all round than the top of a 1.5-litre (2$\frac{1}{2}$-pint) pudding basin.

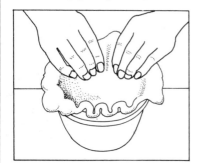

3 Use the rolled-out pastry to line the pudding basin. Put half the butter into the centre with half the sugar.

4 Prick the lemon all over with a skewer. Put the whole lemon on top of the butter and sugar. Add the remaining butter and sugar.

5 Roll out the remaining pastry to a circle to fit the top of the pudding. Dampen the edges and seal the lid. Cover with grease-proof paper and foil.

6 Place over a pan of boiling water and steam for about 4 hours, topping up the water as necessary. Remove paper and turn out on to a warm serving dish. During cooking the lemon inside the pudding bursts and produces a delicious lemon sauce. Each serving should have a piece of the lemon, which will be much softened by the cooking.

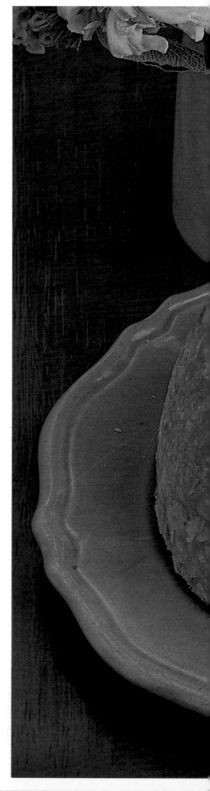

SUSSEX POND PUDDING

An old-fashioned recipe from the south of England, Sussex Pond Pudding takes its name from the fact that during cooking the whole lemon inside bursts, and the resulting juice combines with the other ingredients of butter and sugar to produce a delicious pool or 'pond' of lemon sauce.

Be sure to prick the fruit thoroughly all over with a skewer before placing it inside the suet pastry case—if you do not do this the lemon will remain whole and spoil the finished effect. This pudding is rich enough to be served on its own, but pouring cream can be handed separately for those who like to indulge themselves!

ROLY-POLY WITH HOT JAM SAUCE

2.30	£	499 cals

Serves 4

175 g (6 oz) self raising flour

1.25 ml ($\frac{1}{4}$ tsp) salt

75 g (3 oz) shredded suet

finely grated rind of 1 orange

45–60 ml (3–4 tbsp) hot water

90 ml (6 tbsp) red jam plus 45 ml (3 tbsp)

a little milk

finely grated rind of 1 orange

10 ml (2 tsp) arrowroot

150 ml ($\frac{1}{4}$ pint) fresh orange juice

1 Place the flour and salt into a bowl, then stir in the suet and orange rind. Gradually stir in the hot water until the dough binds together. Form into a ball, turn out on to a floured surface and knead lightly until smooth.

2 Roll out the dough on a floured work surface to a 25 × 20 cm (10 × 8 inch) oblong. Spread the first quantity of jam over the dough to 0.5 cm ($\frac{1}{4}$ inch) of the edges. Brush the edges with milk.

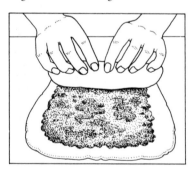

3 Roll up the pastry evenly like a Swiss roll, starting from one short side.

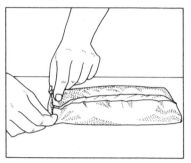

4 Place the roll, seam side down, on a sheet of greased foil measuring at least 35 × 23 cm (12 × 9 inches). Wrap the foil loosely around the roll to allow room for expansion during cooking. Seal well.

5 Place the roly-poly in the top of a steamer over a pan of boiling water and steam for 1$\frac{1}{2}$–2 hours, topping up the water as necessary.

6 Just before serving, make the sauce. Put the remaining jam and orange rind in a heavy-based saucepan. Mix the arrowroot to a paste with a little of the orange juice, then stir the remaining orange juice into the pan. Heat gently until the jam has melted, then stir in the arrowroot paste and bring to the boil. Simmer until thickened, stirring constantly.

7 Unwrap the roly-poly and place on a warmed serving plate. Pour over the hot jam sauce and serve immediately.

SPOTTED DICK

| 2.30 | ▯ | f | 604 cals |

Serves 4

100 g (4 oz) fresh white
  breadcrumbs

75 g (3 oz) self raising flour

pinch of salt

75 g (3 oz) shredded suet

50 g (2 oz) caster sugar

175 g (6 oz) currants

finely grated rind of $\frac{1}{2}$ a lemon

75–90 ml (5–6 tbsp) milk

custard, to serve

1 Place the breadcrumbs, flour, salt, suet, sugar, currants and lemon rind in a bowl. Stir well until thoroughly mixed.

2 Add enough milk to the dry ingredients to bind together, cutting it through with a palette knife until well mixed. Using one hand only, bring the ingredients together to form a soft, slightly sticky dough.

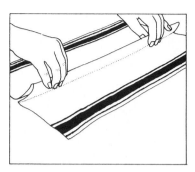

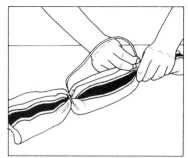

4 Make a 5-cm (2-inch) pleat across a fine-textured, colour-fast teatowel or pudding cloth. Alternatively pleat together sheets of greased, greaseproof paper and strong kitchen foil. Encase the roll in the cloth or foil, pleating the open edges tightly together. Tie the ends securely with string to form a cracker shape. Make a string handle across the top.

5 Lower the suet roll into a large saucepan, two-thirds full of boiling water, curling it if necessary to fit the pan. Cover the pan, lower the heat to a gentle boil and cook for 2 hours. Top up with boiling water at intervals.

6 Lift the spotted dick out of the water. Snip the string and gently roll the pudding on to a serving plate. Decorate with lemon slices if liked and serve immediately, with custard.

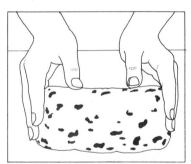

3 Turn the dough out on to a floured work surface. Dust lightly with flour, then knead gently until just smooth. Shape the dough into a neat roll about 15 cm (6 inches) in length.

Milk and Egg Puddings

Milk and eggs are not only two of the most nutritious of ingredients around, they're also immensely versatile. Don't dismiss them as being too basic for anything more than just a plain, everyday pudding. Take a look at the recipes in this chapter, and you'll see that with the addition of a few other ingredients and a little imagination, milk and eggs can make some of the most delicious desserts you've ever tasted.

CRÈME CARAMEL

| 1.25* | 🍶 | 414 cals |

* plus 2 hours cooling, at least 2 hours
chilling and 30 minutes standing time

Serves 4

125 g (4 oz) plus 15 ml (1 tbsp) sugar

150 ml (¼ pint) water

568 ml (1 pint) milk

4 eggs

1.25 ml (¼ tsp) vanilla flavouring
pouring cream, to serve

1 Place the 125 g (4 oz) sugar in a small saucepan and carefully pour in the water. Heat the syrup gently, without boiling, until sugar has dissolved. Stir occasionally.

2 Place a 15-cm (6-inch) soufflé dish in a low oven to warm. Bring the syrup in the pan up to a fast boil and cook rapidly until the syrup starts to brown, shaking the pan to ensure it browns evenly. When caramel is golden, take off heat. Leave for a few seconds.

3 Immediately place the warmed dish on a heatproof surface. Carefully, pour in caramel and leave to cool for 30 minutes.

4 Scald the milk by heating to boiling point. Set aside. Place the eggs in a bowl and add the remaining sugar. Whisk until evenly mixed, then pour on the warm milk. Whisk in the vanilla flavouring, then strain the custard on to caramel. Cover with greased greaseproof paper or foil to prevent a skin forming.

5 Stand the dish in a roasting tin, then pour in enough hot water to come halfway up the sides of the dish. Bake in the oven at 170°C (325°F) mark 3 for about 1½ hours. The custard should be just set and firm to the touch. Insert a skewer in the centre; if clean when withdrawn, the custard is cooked.

6 Take the dish out of the tin and leave to cool for 2 hours. When cold, cover tightly with cling film and refrigerate for 2–3 hours, preferably overnight.

7 To serve, stand at room temperature for 30 minutes. Using the fingertips, gently loosen and ease the edges of the custard away from the dish. Place a rimmed serving dish over the crème caramel and, holding the two dishes firmly, invert.

8 Still holding the dishes together, give a few sharp sideways shakes until the suction is heard to release. Leave the soufflé dish upturned for a few minutes until all the caramel has trickled out. Then ease off and stand in a pan of hot water to soften remaining caramel: pour over the crème caramel, and serve accompanied with cream.

CRÈME BRÛLÉE

1.25* 🗇 £ £ 423 cals

* plus 1 hour cooling and 4–6 hours chilling

Serves 6

600 ml (20 fl oz) whipping cream

4 egg yolks

100 g (4 oz) caster sugar

5 ml (1 tsp) vanilla flavouring

1 Put the cream in the top of a double saucepan or in a heat-proof bowl over a pan of hot water. Heat gently; do not boil.

2 Meanwhile, put the egg yolks, 50 g (2 oz) of the caster sugar and the vanilla flavouring in a bowl and beat thoroughly. Add the cream and mix well together.

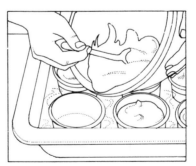

3 Stand six individual ramekin dishes in a roasting tin, then pour in enough hot water to come halfway up the sides of the dishes. Pour the custard mixture slowly into the ramekins, dividing it equally between them.

4 Bake in the oven at 150°C (300°F) mark 2 for about 1 hour or until set, then remove from tin and cool for 1 hour.

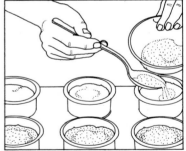

5 Refrigerate for 2–3 hours, preferably overnight. Sprinkle the top of each crème brûlée with the remaining sugar and put under a preheated hot grill for 2–3 minutes until the sugar turns to caramel. Refrigerate again for 2–3 hours before serving.

PANCAKES CREOLE

| 0.45* | 🍴 £ £ ✳* |

| 405–553 cals |

* not including making the pancake batter; freeze cooked pancakes only

Serves 4–6

pancake batter made with 300 ml
 ($\frac{1}{2}$ pint) milk (see page 151)

finely grated rind and juice of 1
 lime

50 g (2 oz) butter or margarine

50 g (2 oz) demerara sugar

60 ml (4 tbsp) dark rum

2.5 ml ($\frac{1}{2}$ tsp) ground cinnamon

3–4 bananas

orange and lime, to decorate

1 Make 8–12 pancakes in the usual way (see page 151). Slide each pancake out of the pan on to a warm plate and stack with greaseproof paper in between.

2 Put the lime rind and juice in a saucepan with the fat, sugar, rum and cinnamon. Heat gently until the fat has melted and the sugar dissolved, stirring occasionally.

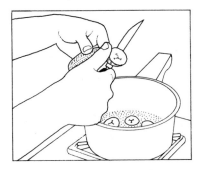

3 Peel the bananas and slice thinly into the sauce. Cook gently for 5 minutes until tender.

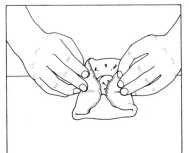

4 Remove the banana slices from the sauce with a slotted spoon. Place a few slices in the centre of each pancake, then fold the pancakes into 'envelopes' around the cooked bananas.

5 Place in a warmed serving dish and pour over the hot sauce. Decorate with orange and lime twists and serve with cream, if liked.

RUM SOUFFLÉ OMELETTE

| 0.20 | 🏠 | £ £ | 513 cals |

Makes 1

2 eggs, separated

5 ml (1 tsp) caster sugar

15 ml (1 tbsp) dark rum

15 g (½ oz) butter

15 ml (1 tbsp) apricot jam,
warmed

30 ml (2 tbsp) icing sugar

hot metal skewers, to decorate
(optional)

1 Put the egg yolks in a bowl with the caster sugar and rum. Mix well together.

2 Whisk the egg whites in a clean dry bowl until they are stiff and standing in peaks.

3 Melt the butter in a heavy-based omelette pan until foaming. Fold the egg whites quickly into the egg yolk mixture, then pour into the foaming butter.

4 Cook over moderate heat for 2–3 minutes until the under-side of the omelette is golden brown, then place the pan under a preheated hot grill and cook for a few minutes more until the top is golden brown.

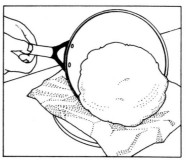

5 Slide the omelette on to a sheet of foil placed on a warmed serving plate. Spread with the warmed jam, then tip the foil to fold over the omelette.

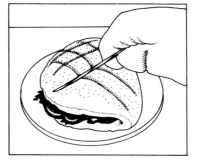

6 Sift the icing sugar thickly over the top of the omelette, then mark in a criss-cross pattern with hot metal skewers, if liked. Remove the foil and serve immediately.

OMELETTE PANS

A good-quality omelette pan is worth investing in if you want to make successful omelettes (both sweet and savoury) every time. The pan should be heavy-based, ideally made from cast iron, copper or enamelled iron. The principle behind this is that the thickness of the base ensures that the egg cooks evenly. Special omelette pans are available, but a heavy-based frying pan with sloping sides and an easy-to-grip handle can be used with equal success.

For a perfect omelette, the egg mixture should not be more than 5 mm (¼ inch) thick, so for a 2- or 3-egg omelette you will need a 15–18 cm (6–7 inch) pan. If the mixture is too thin, the finished omelette will be dry and tough, if too thick, the outside will be overcooked before centre is ready.

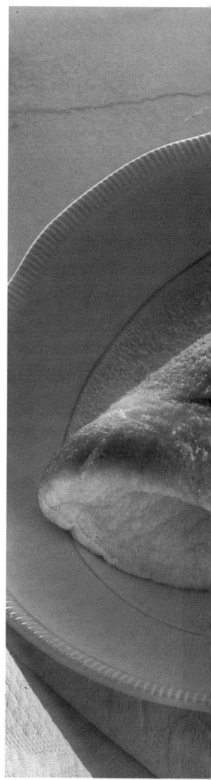

FLOATING ISLANDS

| 0.50* | 🗇 | £ | 412 cals |

* plus 1 hour chilling

Serves 4

5 egg yolks, beaten

450 ml (¾ pint) milk

50 g (2 oz) caster sugar plus 75 ml (5 tbsp)

2.5 ml (½ tsp) vanilla flavouring

1 egg white

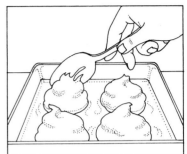

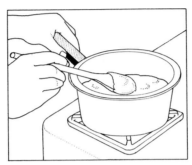

1 Make custard. Put egg yolks, milk and 50 g (2 oz) sugar in the top of a double boiler, or in a heavy-based saucepan over low heat. Cook gently for about 15 minutes, stirring constantly, until the mixture thickens and coats the back of the spoon. Stir in the vanilla flavouring.

2 Divide the custard between four stemmed glasses or dessert dishes. Cover and refrigerate for 1 hour.

3 Meanwhile, whisk the egg white until it will stand in stiff peaks. Add 30 ml (2 tbsp) sugar and whisk again until the sugar is dissolved.

4 Put some cold water into a shallow tin. Bring to a gentle simmer and spoon on the meringue in four even mounds. Poach for about 5 minutes until set, turning once.

5 Remove the meringues with a slotted spoon, drain for a minute on absorbent kitchen paper and spoon on to the custard in the glasses.

6 Put the remaining sugar into a heavy-based saucepan and cook, stirring constantly, for about 3 minutes or until it forms a golden syrup.

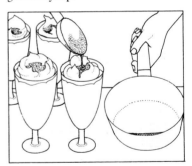

7 Remove from the heat and leave for 2 minutes to cool slightly, then drizzle a little of the warm syrup over the top of each meringue. Serve immediately.

QUEEN OF PUDDINGS

| 1.30 | £ | 306 cals |

Serves 4

450 ml (¾ pint) milk

25 g (1 oz) butter or margarine

finely grated rind of ½ a lemon

2 eggs, separated

50 g (2 oz) caster sugar

75 g (3 oz) fresh white
  breadcrumbs

30 ml (2 tbsp) red jam

1 Put the milk, fat and lemon rind in a saucepan and heat gently. Whisk the egg yolks and half of the sugar lightly and pour on the milk, stirring well.

2 Strain the milk over the breadcrumbs. Pour into a greased 1.1-litre (2-pint) ovenproof dish and leave to stand for 15 minutes.

3 Bake in the oven at 180°C (350°F) mark 4 for 25–30 minutes, until lightly set; remove from the oven.

4 Put the jam in a small saucepan. Warm it over low heat, then spread it over the pudding.

5 Whisk the egg whites until stiff and add half the remaining sugar; whisk again and fold in the remaining sugar.

6 Pile the meringue on top of the jam and bake for a further 15–20 minutes, until the meringue is lightly browned.

QUEEN OF PUDDINGS

Queen of Puddings is a traditional English pudding from the nineteenth century. Original recipes for this homely dish (which can be made entirely from store-cupboard ingredients) used red jam and flavoured the pudding with lemon rind, but you can make your own version according to what ingredients you have to hand. Any kind of jam can be used of course, or orange marmalade or ginger marmalade can be used instead of the jam, and grated orange rind or a little finely chopped stem ginger instead of the lemon. Lemon curd makes a delicious Queen of Puddings, with 25 g (1 oz) desiccated coconut added to the breadcrumb and sugar mixture.

When finishing the pudding with the meringue topping, make absolutely sure that it covers the surface completely and that there are no gaps around the edges for the jam to seep through during baking. After piling the meringue on top, draw it up into peaks with the back of a metal spoon for an attractive effect. Better still, for a neater finish, pipe the meringue on top with a large star nozzle.

APPLE AND BANANA FRITTERS

| 1.00 | 🍞 £ | 218–328 cals |

Serves 4–6

100 g (4 oz) plain flour
pinch of salt
90 ml (6 tbsp) lukewarm water
20 ml (4 tsp) vegetable oil
2 egg whites
1 large cooking apple
2 bananas
juice of ½ a lemon
vegetable oil, for deep frying
caster sugar, to serve

1 Place the flour and salt into a bowl. Make a well in the centre. Add the water and oil and beat to form a smooth batter.

2 Beat the egg whites in a clean dry bowl until they are stiff; then set aside.

3 Peel, quarter and core the apple. Peel the bananas. Slice the fruit thickly and sprinkle at once with the lemon juice to prevent discoloration.

4 Fold the beaten egg whites into the batter, then immediately dip in the slices of fruit.

5 Deep-fry the fritters a few at a time in hot oil until puffed and light golden. Remove with a slotted spoon and pile on to a serving dish lined with absorbent kitchen paper. Serve immediately, sprinkled with caster sugar.

RUM AND COFFEE JUNKET

0.15* f 283 cals

* plus 4 hours setting and 1 hour chilling

Serves 4

568 ml (1 pint) plus 60 ml (4 tbsp) milk—not UHT, long-life or sterilised

30 ml (2 tbsp) caster sugar

10 ml (2 tsp) essence of rennet

10 ml (2 tsp) rum

142 ml (5 fl oz) soured cream

10 ml (2 tsp) coffee and chicory essence

plain and white chocolate, to decorate

1 Put the 568 ml (1 pint) milk in a saucepan and heat until just warm to the finger.

2 Add the sugar, rennet and rum and stir until the sugar has dissolved.

3 Pour the mixture at once into four individual dishes or a 900-ml (1½-pint) shallow, edged serving dish. Put in a warm place, undisturbed, for 4 hours to set.

4 Lightly whisk the soured cream. Gradually add the 60 ml (4 tbsp) milk and the coffee essence, whisking until smooth.

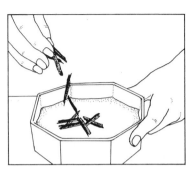

5 Carefully flood the top of the junket with the coffee cream, taking care not to disturb the junket. Decorate with pared or coarsely grated chocolate. Refrigerate for 1 hour.

CREMA FRITTA

1.25*	🍴	314–471 cals

* plus 2–3 hours cooling

Serves 4–6

3 eggs

50 g (2 oz) caster sugar

50 g (2 oz) plain flour

225 ml (8 fl oz) milk

300 ml (10 fl oz) single cream

finely grated rind of ½ a lemon

100 g (4 oz) dry white breadcrumbs

vegetable oil, for frying

caster sugar, to serve

1 In a large bowl, beat 2 eggs and the sugar together until the mixture is pale.

2 Add the flour, beating all the time, and then, very slowly, beat in the milk and cream. Add the lemon rind.

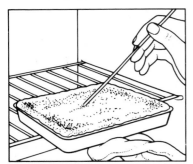

3 Pour the mixture into a buttered shallow 18-cm (7-inch) square cake tin. Bake in the oven at 180°C (350°F) mark 4 for about 1 hour, until a skewer inserted in the middle comes out clean. Leave to cool for 2–3 hours, preferably overnight.

4 When completely cold, cut into sixteen cubes and remove from the cake tin.

5 Beat the remaining egg in a bowl. Dip the cubes in the egg and then in the breadcrumbs until well coated.

6 Heat the oil in a frying pan and when hot, slide in the cubes. Fry for 2–3 minutes until golden brown and a crust is formed. Turn and fry the second side. Drain well on absorbent kitchen paper. Serve immediately, sprinkled with caster sugar.

CREMA FRITTA

Literally translated, this simple Italian dessert means 'fried cream', which is in fact exactly what it is—a thick creamy sauce which is baked, chilled and cut into squares, then fried in oil until crisp and golden.

In Italy, it is traditional to celebrate *Carnevale*—the day before Lent—by eating *crema fritta*. Children and young people invite friends home and everyone eats *crema fritta* in the way that people in other countries eat pancakes. Sprinkled liberally with white sugar, they are always eaten informally—with the fingers.

PRALINE ICE CREAM

0.50* ☐ £ £ ✳ 393 cals

* plus 45 minutes cooling, 9 hours freezing and 30 minutes softening

Serves 6

50 g (2 oz) whole unblanched almonds

50 g (2 oz) granulated sugar

300 ml (½ pint) milk

1 vanilla pod

1 egg

2 egg yolks

75 g (3 oz) caster sugar

200 ml (7 fl oz) double cream

coarsely grated plain chocolate, to decorate (optional)

1 Place the almonds and granulated sugar in a heavy-based pan. Heat slowly until the sugar caramelises, turning occasionally.

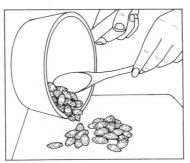

2 Pour the mixture on to an oiled baking sheet to cool and harden for about 15 minutes.

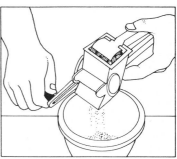

3 Use a mouli grater, blender or food processor to grind the cooled praline to a powder.

4 Bring the milk and vanilla pod to the boil, take off the heat and leave to infuse for 15 minutes.

5 Beat the egg, egg yolks and caster sugar until pale in colour, strain in the milk, stir, and return to the saucepan. Cook slowly for about 10 minutes until the custard coats the back of a wooden spoon—do not boil. Cool completely for 30–40 minutes. Lightly whip the cream and fold into the custard.

6 Freeze the mixture for about 3 hours until mushy. Beat well, then fold in the praline powder. Spoon into a freezer container and freeze for about 6 hours until firm.

7 Transfer to the refrigerator to soften for 30 minutes before serving. Serve scooped into glasses and decorated with coarsely grated chocolate, if liked.

PRALINE

Praline is a French confection made by cooking almonds and sugar together until the sugar caramelises, then crushing the set mixture to a powder. This recipe for Praline Ice Cream uses white praline, although brown praline can also be used. Brown praline has a stronger flavour than white; they are both made in exactly the same way, the only difference is that for brown praline almonds in their skins are used, whereas white praline uses blanched almonds.

FROZEN BRANDY CREAMS

| 0.30* | 🍱 £ £ ✳ | 423 cals |

* plus 30 minutes cooling and 5 hours freezing

Serves 4

4 egg yolks

150 g (5 oz) caster sugar

90 ml (6 tbsp) brandy

150 ml (5 fl oz) double cream

coffee dragées, to decorate

1 Place the egg yolks, caster sugar and brandy in a deep, medium-sized heatproof bowl. Using a wooden spoon, stir well.

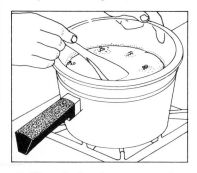

2 Place the bowl over a pan of simmering water; the bowl base should not touch the water. Stir the mixture all the time for about 15 minutes, until it thickens slightly and will just coat the back of the spoon. Do not overheat or the eggs may curdle. Take off heat and cool for 30 minutes.

3 Lightly whip the cream and stir half into the cold brandy mixture. Pour into four small soufflé or ramekin dishes. Freeze for at least 5 hours, until firm.

4 To serve, decorate each ramekin with a whirl of the remaining whipped cream, then top with a coffee dragée. Serve immediately.

TEA CREAM

0.45* ▯ £ £ 293 cals

* plus 2–3 hours setting

Serves 4

300 ml (½ pint) milk

15 g (½ oz) Earl Grey tea

2 eggs, separated

30 ml (2 tbsp) caster sugar

45 ml (3 tbsp) water

15 ml (3 tsp) gelatine

150 ml (5 fl oz) double cream

2 Beat the egg yolks with the sugar, then strain on the milk and mix well. Return to the pan and cook gently for 10 minutes, stirring all the time, until the custard thickens slightly and just coats the back of the spoon.

3 Put the water in a small heat-proof bowl and sprinkle in the gelatine. Stand the bowl over a saucepan of hot water and heat gently until dissolved. Mix into the tea mixture, then leave for about 2 hours until beginning to set. Stir the mixture occasionally.

4 Whip the cream until thick but not stiff, then fold into the custard. Finally, whisk the egg whites until stiff and fold into the mixture.

5 Pour the cream mixture into a dampened 600-ml (1-pint) mould and refrigerate for about 2–3 hours until set. Turn out on to a chilled dish to serve.

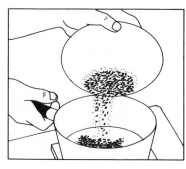

1 Put the milk into a saucepan, add the tea and bring to the boil. Remove from the heat and leave to infuse for 10–15 minutes, or until the milk is well coloured with the tea.

TEA CREAM

Earl Grey tea, a blended black tea flavoured with bergamot oil, gives this unusual tea cream a subtle, perfumed flavour.

It isn't essential to use Earl Grey, however, you can use any of your favourite Ceylon or China teas, although aromatic teas are more flavoursome in cooking. Why not try jasmine tea, lapsang souchong or orange pekoe?

TUTTI FRUTTI ICE CREAM

| 0.45* | 🍴 | ££ | ✳ | 475–593 cals |

* plus 2–3 hours soaking, 30 minutes cooling and 5 hours freezing

Serves 8–10

| 90 ml (6 tbsp) dark rum |
| 50 g (2 oz) sultanas |
| 50 g (2 oz) stoned dates |
| 50 g (2 oz) glacé cherries |
| 50 g (2 oz) dried plump apricots |
| 568 ml (1 pint) milk |
| 1 vanilla pod or a few drops of vanilla flavouring |
| 6 egg yolks |
| 175 g (6 oz) caster sugar |
| 600 ml (20 fl oz) double cream |

1 Pour the rum into a screw-top jar or a bowl. Add the sultanas, then roughly snip the dates, cherries and apricots into the jar or bowl. Make sure all the fruit is coated with rum. Cover and leave to macerate for 2–3 hours shaking or tossing occasionally until the rum is absorbed.

2 Meanwhile, make the ice cream. Put the milk and vanilla pod or flavouring into a heavy-based saucepan and bring almost to the boil. Remove from the heat, cover and leave to infuse for 15 minutes.

3 Beat the egg yolks and sugar together in a bowl until thick and pale, stir in the milk and strain back into the saucepan.

4 Cook the custard gently over a low heat, stirring all the time, until it coats the back of a wooden spoon. Do not boil or it will curdle. Cover and leave the custard for about 30 minutes until completely cold.

5 Pour into a chilled, shallow freezer container and freeze for about 2 hours until mushy.

6 Turn the frozen mixture into a large, chilled basin and mash with a whisk or fork.

7 Lightly whip the cream and fold into the mixture with the macerated fruit. Return to the freezer and freeze for 3 hours, or until required, until firm.

8 Allow to soften for about 30 minutes in the refrigerator before serving.

——————— VARIATION ———————

For a short-cut version of this ice cream, you can use a 425 g (15 oz) can of custard instead of making the egg custard as here. With vanilla flavouring added and the heady flavour of fruit macerated in rum, no-one will guess the custard came out of a can! If you are making the ice cream with children in mind, add 25 g (1 oz) chocolate polka dots to the mixture in stage 7 when adding the macerated fruit.

Fruit Desserts

There's nothing to compare with fresh fruits for making delicious desserts in next to no time. The beautiful colours of fresh fruit such as oranges, apples, peaches, raspberries, redcurrants and strawberries attract the eye and titillate the palate—even with those who say they don't have a sweet tooth. It's the natural sweet simplicity of a fresh fruit dessert that's far more appealing—and satisfying—than any elaborate concoction.

ORANGES IN CARAMEL

| 0.30* | 🍴 | £ | 155–310 cals |

* plus 2–3 hours chilling

Serves 4–8

8 medium juicy oranges

225 g (8 oz) caster sugar

30 ml (2 tbsp) orange-flavoured liqueur

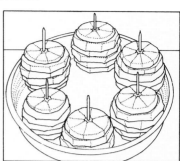

1 Thinly pare the rind from 2 oranges, keeping it free of white pith. Cut the rind into very thin julienne strips with scissors or a sharp knife. Place in a small saucepan and cover well with water. Cover the pan and cook for 5 minutes until the rind is tender. Drain and rinse under cold running water.

2 Cut away all the pith from these oranges and both rind and pith from the remaining oranges. (Reserve any juice that may be squeezed out from the oranges as you do this.)

3 Slice the orange flesh into rounds, discarding any pips, and arrange in a serving dish. If liked, the orange rounds can be re-assembled in the shape of the orange. Secure each with a wooden cocktail stick, then arrange in the serving dish.

4 Place the sugar and 300 ml ($\frac{1}{2}$ pint) water in a saucepan and heat gently until the sugar has dissolved. Bring to the boil and boil until caramel coloured. Remove the pan from the heat, add 45 ml (3 tbsp) water and return it to a low heat to dissolve the caramel. Add the reserved orange juice and the liqueur.

5 Leave the caramel syrup to cool for 2–3 minutes, then pour over the oranges. Top with the julienne strips. Refrigerate for 2–3 hours, turning the oranges occasionally, before serving.

VARIATIONS

For a sweet, crunchy topping to this classic orange dessert, make caramel chips: dissolve 75 g (3 oz) granulated sugar very gently in 75 ml (3 fl oz) water. Increase the heat and boil rapidly without stirring until the syrup turns a rich-brown caramel colour. Pour at once into a greased shallow tin (a Swiss roll tin is ideal), then leave until cold and set. Crush with a mallet or rolling pin into fine pieces and sprinkle over the oranges just before serving (not before or the caramel will go soft).

CHERRY PIE

Pictured on cover

1.00*	✳	449–674 cals

* plus 30 minutes chilling

Serves 4–6

700 g (1½ lb) fresh red or black cherries

100 g (4 oz) sugar

30 ml (2 tbsp) plain flour

15 ml (1 tbsp) water

5 ml (1 tsp) kirsch (optional)

225 g (8 oz) shortcrust pastry (see page 155)

caster sugar, to dredge

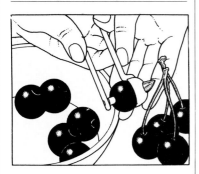

1 Stone the cherries, but keep them as whole as possible. Then mix the sugar and flour together and layer the cherries and sugar mixture in a 20.5-cm (8-inch) pie plate. Sprinkle over the water and kirsch, if using.

2 Roll out the pastry on a floured work surface to a shape 5 cm (2 inches) wider than the pie plate. Dampen the rim of the pie dish, then cut a 2.5-cm (1-inch) strip from the outer edge of the pastry and press on to the rim. Dampen the pastry rim and cover with pastry lid, sealing edges well. Trim the use pastry trimmings, to decorate. Chill for 30 minutes.

3 Make a hole in the centre of the pastry. Bake in the oven at 200°C (400°F) mark 6 for 25–30 minutes until the pastry is lightly browned and the fruit is cooked. Sprinkle immediately with caster sugar and serve warm.

TARTE TATIN

1.00*	⬦	f	✳	379 cals

* plus 30 minutes chilling

Serves 8

150 g (5 oz) butter or block margarine

175 g (6 oz) plain flour

65 g (2½ oz) caster sugar

1 egg yolk

15 ml (1 tbsp) water

450 g (1 lb) crisp eating apples

whipped cream, to serve

1 Rub 125 g (4 oz) fat into the flour until the mixture resembles fine breadcrumbs. Add 15 g (½ oz) caster sugar. Blend the egg yolk with the water and stir into the mixture. Knead the dough lightly, then refrigerate while making the filling.

2 In a saucepan, melt the remaining fat and add the remaining caster sugar. Heat until caramelised and golden brown. Remove from the heat and pour into a 20.5-cm (8-inch) round sandwich tin.

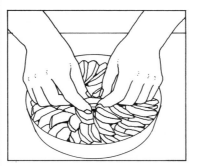

3 Peel, core and halve the apples and slice them into 1-cm (½-inch) pieces. Pack them tightly to fill the bottom of the tin, leaving no gaps.

4 Roll out the pastry on a floured work surface to a round slightly larger than the tin. Place on top of the apples and tuck in around the edges of the tin. Refrigerate for 30 minutes.

5 Place the tin on a baking sheet and bake in the oven at 200°C (400°F) mark 6 for 30–35 minutes until the pastry is golden. Turn out, apple side uppermost, on to a serving dish. Serve hot, with a bowl of cream.

TARTE TATIN

Correctly called *Tarte des Demoiselles Tatin* in French, this famous upside-down apple tart is named after the sisters Tatin, hoteliers in the nineteenth century who originated the recipe.

There are now numerous versions of the original recipe, which has become something of a classic in French cookery. Most recipes use shortcrust pastry as here, although some use puff, but in all versions the pastry is baked on the top so that the apples are completely sealed in with their juices, then the tart turned out upside down for serving. In France, *crème fraîche* is usually served with warm tarte Tatin; it is slightly more acidic than our fresh cream, which makes a good contrast with the sweetness of the caramelised apples. Alternatively, serve with cream.

Rhubarb and Orange Chiffon Pie

0.45* £ ✳ 589 cals

* plus 1 hour cooling and at least 2 hours chilling

Serves 4

150 g (6 oz) digestive biscuits, crushed

50 g (2 oz) demerara sugar

75 g (3 oz) unsalted butter, melted

560-g (1 lb 4-oz) can rhubarb, drained

finely grated rind and juice of 1 large orange

2 eggs, separated

50 g (2 oz) caster sugar

30 ml (2 tbsp) cornflour

2.5 ml ($\frac{1}{2}$ tsp) ground ginger

orange slices, to decorate

1 In a bowl, mix together the crushed biscuits and demerara sugar, then stir in the melted unsalted butter.

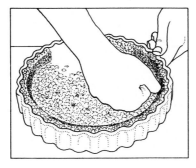

2 Press the mixture over the base and sides of a 20.5-cm (8-inch) fluted flan dish. Chill in the refrigerator while preparing the filling.

3 Work the rhubarb to a purée in an electric blender. Put the orange rind and juice into a heavy-based saucepan. Add the egg yolks, caster sugar, cornflour and ground ginger. Heat gently, stirring constantly, until thick. Stir into the rhubarb purée.

4 Whisk the egg whites until stiff. Fold into the rhubarb custard, then spoon the mixture into the biscuit crust. Refrigerate for at least 4 hours, or overnight. Decorate with orange slices just before serving.

--- VARIATIONS ---

Chiffon pies are American in origin, and there are many different recipes, but perhaps the most famous is lemon chiffon pie. All chiffon pies are made with beaten egg white; usually the egg white is folded into a base of custard or fruit, although sometimes it is spread over the top rather like a meringue pie. If you prefer a warm, baked pie, then pop this rhubarb and orange chiffon pie into a preheated 200°C (400°F) mark 6 oven for 10 minutes before decorating with the oranges.

If you want to use fresh rhubarb rather than canned as here, you will need to poach 450 g (1 lb) with sugar and a little water beforehand and drain off the juice before using.

RØDGRØD

0.35*	£	✳	339–452 cals

* plus 10 minutes cooling and 30 minutes chilling

Serves 6–8

450 g (1 lb) fresh redcurrants or 425-g (15-oz) can, drained

450 g (1 lb) fresh raspberries or 425-g (15-oz) can, drained

45 ml (3 tbsp) arrowroot

225–350 g (8–12 oz) caster sugar, if using fresh fruit

25 g (1 oz) blanched almonds and whipped cream, to decorate

1 Place the fresh fruits in a saucepan with 60 ml (4 tbsp) water. Simmer gently for about 20 minutes or until really soft.

2 Purée in a blender or food processor until smooth, then push through a nylon sieve. If using canned fruit, push through a sieve.

3 Blend a little of the purée with the arrowroot, put the rest into a saucepan and bring slowly to boiling point. Stir into the blended mixture, then return it all to the pan. Bring to the boil again, cook for 2–3 minutes and sweeten to taste if using fresh fruit. Leave to cool for 10 minutes.

4 Shred the almonds into thin strips with a sharp knife. Toast them lightly under the grill. Cool for 5 minutes.

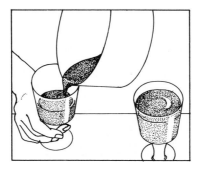

5 Pour the rødgrød into individual tall or shallow glasses and refrigerate for 30 minutes. Top with whipped cream and the shredded almonds just before serving.

RØDGRØD

Rødgrød is a Danish dessert which is best described as a fruit soup. It is always made with fresh soft summer fruit: redcurrants and raspberries are used in our version, although blackcurrants, blackberries, strawberries, cherries and even rhubarb can be used, depending on what is available. The important thing is to mix at least two of these fruits together to provide good flavour and colour.

Such fruit soups are popular all over Scandinavia, and are sometimes even eaten as a starter, either hot or cold. In Finland, they are called *kiisseli*, and are often made with more unusual soft red fruits such as bilberries, cloudberries and cranberries.

This recipe for rødgrød is refreshingly simple, whereas some recipes use spices such as cinnamon and the thinly pared zest of citrus fruit—you can add these too if you wish. Fresh whipped cream to serve is traditional, or you can use soured cream or natural yogurt, in which case the soup will look most attractive if the cream or yogurt is swirled over the top just before serving.

POIRES BELLE HÉLÈNE

 2.00 ▯ £ £ 357 cals

Serves 6

100 g (4 oz) sugar

900 ml (1½ pints) water

thinly pared rind and juice of 2
  oranges

6 cooking pears (preferably
  Conference)

225 g (8 oz) plain chocolate, broken
  into pieces

60 ml (4 tbsp) orange-flavoured
  liqueur

orange slices, to decorate

1 Put the sugar, water and half
  the orange rind in a large
heavy-based saucepan and heat
gently, without stirring, until the
sugar has dissolved.

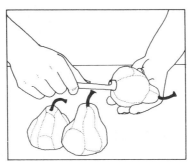

2 Meanwhile, peel the pears
  quickly (to prevent discoloration), leaving the stalks on.
Cut out the cores from the bottom
and level them so that the pears
will stand upright.

3 Stand the pears in the syrup,
  cover the pan and simmer
gently for 20 minutes or until
tender. Remove from the heat and
leave to cool, covered tightly.
Spoon the syrup over the pears
occasionally during cooling.

4 Meanwhile, make the decoration. Cut the remaining
orange rind into thin matchstick
(julienne) strips. Blanch in boiling
water for 2 minutes, then drain
and immediately refresh under
cold running water. Leave to drain
on absorbent kitchen paper.

5 Make the chocolate sauce. Put
  the chocolate and liqueur in a
heatproof bowl standing over a
pan of gently simmering water.
Heat gently until chocolate melts.

6 Remove the pears from the
  syrup, stand on a large serving
dish, or 6 individual dishes and
chill for 2 hours. Discard the
orange rind from the syrup. Stir
the melted chocolate into 150 ml
(¼ pint) of the syrup with the
orange juice, then slowly bring to
the boil, stirring constantly.
Simmer, stirring, until the sauce
is thick and syrupy.

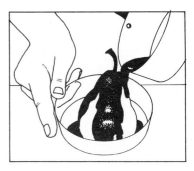

7 To serve, pour the hot
  chocolate sauce over the cold
pears and sprinkle with the orange
julienne. Decorate with orange
slices and serve immediately.

115

CITRUS SOUFFLÉ

| 1.30* | 🍳 | £ £ | ✳ | 290–386 cals |

* plus 4 hours setting

Serves 6–8

finely grated rind and juice of 1 lemon

finely grated rind and juice of 1 orange

juice of 1 grapefruit

15 ml (3 tsp) gelatine

4 eggs, separated

100 g (4 oz) caster sugar

300 ml (10 fl oz) double cream

crushed sweet biscuits and crystallised oranges and lemons, to decorate

1 Prepare an 18-cm (6-inch) soufflé dish. Cut a double thickness of greaseproof paper long enough to go around the outside of the dish and 5–7.5 cm (2–3 inches) deeper. Secure around the outside with paper clips and string.

2 Pour the fruit juices into a heatproof bowl and sprinkle in the gelatine. Stand the bowl over a saucepan of hot water and heat gently until dissolved. Remove the bowl from the water and set aside to cool for 45 minutes.

3 Put the fruit rinds, egg yolks and sugar in a large heatproof bowl and stand over the pan of gently simmering water. Whisk until the mixture is thick and holds a ribbon trail.

4 Remove the bowl from the pan and whisk in the gelatine liquid. Leave until beginning to set, whisking occasionally.

5 Whip the cream until it will stand in soft peaks. Whisk the egg whites until stiff. Fold the cream into the soufflé, then the egg whites, until evenly blended.

6 Pour the mixture into the prepared soufflé dish and level the surface. Chill in the refrigerator for at least 4 hours until set.

7 Carefully remove the paper from the edge of the soufflé. Press the crushed biscuits around the exposed edge, then decorate the top with crystallised fruit. Serve chilled.

─────────── VARIATIONS ───────────

Children love the zingy flavour of this soufflé, and if you don't want to go to the trouble of preparing a soufflé dish with a collar, it can be set in a serving bowl like a mousse. Ring the changes with the flavour according to the fruit available — make it with just oranges and lemons if you like, or with just one citrus fruit. For an extra special dinner party, add a spoonful or two of orange-flavoured liqueur.

BRANDIED STUFFED APRICOTS

0.35*	f	274 cals

* plus 50 minutes cooling and 2–3 hours chilling

Serves 4

16 small apricots

120 ml (8 tbsp) apricot brandy

30 ml (2 tbsp) caster sugar

finely grated rind and juice of 1 lemon

150 ml ($\frac{1}{4}$ pint) water

125 g (5 oz) cottage cheese

50 g (2 oz) full fat soft cheese

15 ml (1 tbsp) icing sugar, sifted

chopped toasted hazelnuts, to decorate

1 Place the apricots in a saucepan with the brandy, caster sugar, 15 ml (1 tbsp) lemon juice and the water. Poach gently for about 15 minutes until just tender. Remove apricots and leave to cool for 30 minutes.

2 Bring the poaching liquid to the boil, bubble for 2–3 minutes until well reduced and syrupy. Leave to cool for 20 minutes.

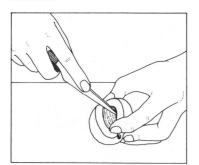

3 Using a sharp knife, skin the apricots. Slice almost in half and remove the kernel.

4 Sieve the cottage cheese into a bowl, add the full fat soft cheese, icing sugar and grated lemon rind and beat together until well mixed.

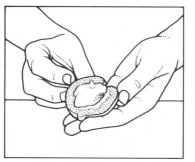

5 Sandwich the apricots together with a little of the cheese mixture. Divide the apricots between four individual glass dishes.

6 Spoon a little of the cooled syrup over the apricots, then sprinkle with chopped nuts. Refrigerate for 2–3 hours before serving.

APRICOTS

Apricots originated in China, but are now grown all over the world, wherever the weather is kind enough to ripen this delicate stone fruit. Smaller and more unusual than its relations the nectarine and peach, the apricot is highly prized for its unique flavour and aroma. Fresh apricots do not keep well, however, and their season is relatively short compared to other stone fruit; most apricots go for canning and drying (dried Hunza apricots from Afghanistan are a great luxury) or for jam making and preserves.

If fresh apricots are not available, this recipe can be made with small peaches or nectarines, but as these are always larger than apricots you will only need half the quantity, thus allowing two fruits per person. Ordinary brandy can be substituted for apricot or peach brandy.

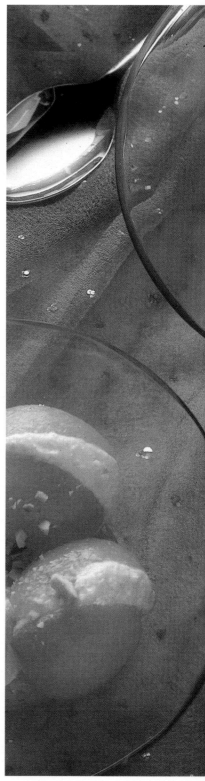

PINEAPPLE AND BANANA FLAMBÉ

| 0.50 | £ £ | 235–313 cals |

Serves 6–8

| 1 medium pineapple |
| 900 g (2 lb) firm bananas |
| 125 g (4 oz) dried figs |
| 50 g (2 oz) butter or margarine |
| 125 g (4 oz) demerara sugar |
| 45 ml (3 tbsp) lemon juice |
| 2.5 ml ($\frac{1}{2}$ tsp) ground mixed spice |
| 60 ml (4 tbsp) dark rum |

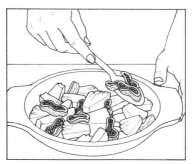

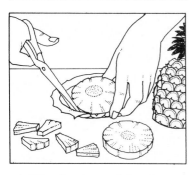

1 Slice the pineapple into 1-cm ($\frac{1}{2}$-inch) pieces. Snip off the skin and cut the flesh into chunks, discarding the core.

2 Peel and thickly slice the bananas into the bottom of a shallow ovenproof dish; spoon the pineapple on top.

3 Cut the figs into coarse shreds and scatter over the fruit. Then put the butter, sugar, strained lemon juice and spice together in a saucepan and heat until well blended; pour over the prepared fruit.

4 Cover tightly and bake in the oven at 200°C (400°F) mark 6 for 25 minutes until the fruit is tender.

5 Heat the rum gently in a small saucepan, remove from the heat and ignite with a match. Pour immediately over the fruit and bring the dish to the table while still flaming.

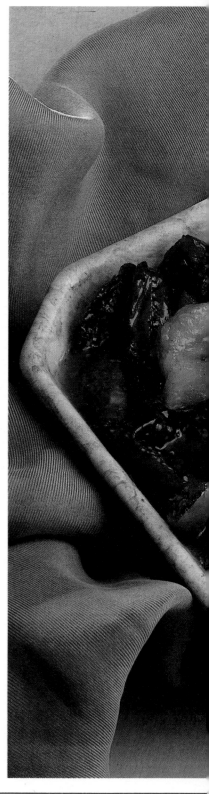

SERVING IDEA

For a special occasion such as a dinner party, you can serve this dessert in the pineapple shells. It will look really spectacular if carried flaming to the table, and any mixture which will not fit into the pineapple shells can be served separately in a fruit bowl.

To make two pineapple shells from one pineapple: with a large, sharp knife, slice the pineapple in half lengthways, cutting right through the crown and base. Insert the blade of a long, ser-rated knife into the flesh of one pineapple half, about 5 mm ($\frac{1}{4}$ inch) in from the edge of the shell, and cut all around the inside. Cut through the flesh in parallel lines, first lengthways and then crossways to produce squares of flesh (take care not to cut through the skin at the base). Scoop out the flesh with a sharp-edged teaspoon. Repeat with the second pineapple half, then turn both shells upside-down and leave to drain before filling.

RASPBERRY PARFAIT

0.30* ☐ £ £ ✳ 351 cals

* plus 2–3 hours freezing and 30 minutes softening

Serves 6

450 g (1 lb) fresh raspberries, hulled

75 g (3 oz) icing sugar, sifted

75 g (3 oz) granulated sugar

100 ml (4 fl oz) water

2 egg whites

15 ml (1 tbsp) kirsch or raspberry-flavoured liqueur (optional)

squeeze of lemon juice

300 ml (10 fl oz) double cream

fresh mint leaves, to decorate

1 Purée the raspberries in a blender or food processor, then push through a sieve to remove the pips. Stir icing sugar into purée.

2 Put the granulated sugar and water into a heavy-based saucepan and dissolve over gentle heat.

3 When dissolved, bring to the boil and boil until slightly tacky. Remove from the heat.

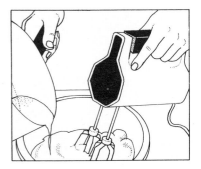

4 Whisk the egg whites until very stiff, then pour the hot sugar syrup on to them, whisking until thick, shiny and mousse-like. Leave for 10 minutes until cool.

5 Flavour the raspberry purée with the liqueur, if using, and the lemon juice. Fold into the meringue mixture.

6 Lightly whip the cream and fold into the raspberry mixture. Taste for sweetness and add more sugar if necessary. Pour into a chilled shallow freezer container and freeze for 3–4 hours until the mixture is firm.

7 Allow the raspberry parfait to soften for 30 minutes in the refrigerator before serving. Decorate with the mint leaves.

PARFAIT

The term *parfait* can be confusing. Originally it was used to describe an iced coffee cream, but nowadays the term is often used in restaurants to describe any fancy ice cream—usually the type that has been set in a bombe mould. Strictly speaking, a parfait should be made from a mousse-like mixture such as this one in which a hot sugar syrup is mixed with beaten egg whites, then enriched with cream.

KIWI FRUIT SORBET

0.30* £ ✳ 103 cals

* plus 30 minutes cooling and 6 hours freezing

Serves 6

50 g (2 oz) sugar

150 ml (¼ pint) water

6 kiwi fruit

2 egg whites

slices of kiwi fruit, to decorate

orange-flavoured liqueur and wafers, to serve

1 Place the sugar in saucepan with the water. Heat gently until the sugar dissolves, then simmer for 2 minutes. Cool for 30 minutes.

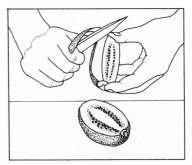

2 Halve the kiwi fruit and peel thinly or pull away the skins without damaging the flesh.

3 Place the fruit in a blender or food processor with the cool syrup. Work to a smooth purée, then pass through a nylon sieve to remove the pips. Pour into a chilled shallow freezer container. Freeze for 2 hours until mushy.

4 Beat the mixture with a fork to break down any ice crystals.

5 Whisk the egg whites until stiff, then fold through the fruit mixture until evenly blended. Return to freezer for 4 hours.

6 Scoop into individual glass dishes, decorate and spoon over some liqueur. Serve with wafers.

FRUDITÉS

0.20	£ £	245 cals

Serves 6

150 ml (5 fl oz) double cream

142 ml (5 fl oz) soured cream

30 ml (2 tbsp) icing sugar, sifted

225 g (8 oz) apricots

225 g (8 oz) strawberries

175 g (6 oz) black or green grapes

2 crisp eating apples

2 bananas

juice of 1 lemon

3 Halve the grapes if they are not the seedless variety and flick out the seeds.

4 Quarter and core the apples, but do not peel them. Peel the bananas and cut into 4-cm (1½-inch) chunks.

5 Arrange the fruit on individual serving plates and sprinkle immediately with lemon juice to prevent discoloration.

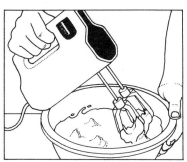

1 First prepare the dip. Whip the two creams together with the icing sugar until standing in soft peaks. Pipe or spoon into six individual dishes.

2 Prepare the fruit. Halve and stone the apricots. Wash the strawberries under cold running water, but do not hull them.

6 Place the dishes of cream dip next to the fruit and serve immediately. Use fingers or small fondue forks to dunk the fruit into the cream dip.

FRUDITÉS

This is a sweet version of the French starter *crudités* which consists of fresh raw vegetables served with a vinaigrette dressing or mayonnaise-type dip. Instead of vegetables, frudités uses raw fresh fruit served with a sweet creamy dip! And it's as much fun for your guests as a fondue party if you provide forks for dipping the fruit into the dressing. Frudités can be made at any time of year, with whatever fruit happens to be in season. As long as the fruit is in peak condition and the combination of different types interesting, the dish is bound to be a success.

In the winter, when fruit is scarce and more expensive, you can cut up squares of plain home-made cake (such as Genoese sponge or Madeira) to help bulk up the quantity of fruit. And if you are entertaining children amongst your guests, they would appreciate a chocolate sauce to dip their fruit into—either make a hot chocolate sauce as you would for ice cream, or use a commercial variety if time is short.

MANDARIN AND LYCHEE MOUSSE

0.45* £ ✳ 292 cals

* plus 30 minutes cooling and at least
2 hours setting

Serves 6

3 eggs, separated

2 egg yolks

75 g (3 oz) caster sugar

298-g (10½-oz) can mandarin
   oranges in natural juice

310-g (11-oz) can lychees in syrup

15 ml (3 tsp) gelatine

150 ml (5 fl oz) double cream

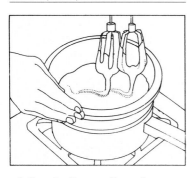

1 Put the 5 egg yolks and sugar
in a large heatproof bowl and
stand over a saucepan of gently
simmering water. Whisk until the
mixture is thick and holds a
ribbon trail, then remove the bowl
from the pan. Leave for 30
minutes, whisking occasionally.

2 Reserve 60 ml (4 tbsp) of the
mandarin juice. Purée half the
oranges and the remaining juice in
a blender or food processor with
the lychees and half the syrup.

3 Put the reserved mandarin
syrup in a heatproof bowl and
sprinkle in the gelatine. Stand the
bowl over a saucepan of hot water
and heat gently until dissolved.
Remove the bowl from the pan
and leave to cool slightly.

4 Stir the mandarin purée into
the cooled egg yolk mixture,
then stir in the gelatine liquid
until evenly mixed.

5 Whip the cream until standing
in soft peaks. Whisk the egg
whites until stiff. Fold first the
cream and then the egg whites into
the mousse until evenly blended.
Turn into a glass serving bowl and
chill for at least 2 hours until set.

6 When the mousse is set serve
decorated with the reserved
mandarin oranges and extra
whipped cream, if liked.

LYCHEES

The tree fruit lychee (lichee or
litchi as it is also known) originated in China, but it is now
grown in tropical countries else-
where in the world. Canned
peeled lychees, with their trans-
lucent white flesh, are readily
available. The skin of a lychee is
a most attractive reddish brown
with a rough almost brittle
texture, but the fresh fruit is
rarely seen outside specialist
markets. The unique perfumed
flavour of lychees, and their
beautifully smooth texture,
makes them an interesting ingredient to include in a mousse
such as the one on this page.

PRUNE AND PORT FOOL

| 0.45* | £ | ✳ | 433 cals |

* plus overnight soaking and 2 hours chilling

Serves 4

100 g (4 oz) stoned prunes, soaked overnight in cold water

50 g (2 oz) caster sugar

60 ml (4 tbsp) port

finely grated rind and juice of 1 medium orange

150 ml (¼ pint) thick custard, cooled

150 ml (5 fl oz) double cream

sweet biscuits, to serve

1 Drain the prunes, then put in a saucepan with the sugar, port, orange rind and juice. Simmer for about 15 minutes until soft. Leave to cool slightly, then purée in a blender or food processor. Leave to cool completely.

2 Fold the cooled custard into the puréed prunes. Whip the cream until it will stand in soft peaks, then fold into the prune custard until evenly blended.

3 Divide the mixture between four individual glasses, then chill in the refrigerator for about 2 hours until firm. Serve chilled, with sweet biscuits.

USEFUL INFORMATION
AND
BASIC RECIPES

Basic Equipment

Whether making an elaborate dessert for a dinner party, or whipping up a simple pudding to end a family meal, having the right equipment is all-important. Not only will it make your task much easier, but it will also greatly improve the results, in terms of both flavour and appearance — many desserts, for example, can be made in attractive moulds and then turned out, to offer pretty and unusual shapes.

BASIC EQUIPMENT

Most desserts and puddings can be made without anything other than good basic kitchen equipment. However, there are a number of pans and dishes which will help make desserts look more attractive and be more authentic.

Pans and dishes come in different materials. Good-quality pans should last a lifetime if treated with care. Aluminium pans are excellent for baking as the metal is a good conductor of heat; pans with non-stick surfaces are easily cleaned. Ceramic dishes are good for puddings and pies which must be served straight from the oven. Thick ceramic dishes are also good when baking slowly such as with custards. Pans with removable bases make it easier to remove the flan or cake.

Use the size of pan specified in the recipe. Too large a pan and the mixture may cook too quickly or it may not rise properly. On the other hand, if the pan is too small the mixture may not cook evenly and will produce an uneven texture and an over browned surface.

If necessary use a pan which is too large rather than too small and reduce the cooking time by about 5–10 minutes. Chilled desserts made in the wrong pan size may look misshapen and out of proportion.

BASINS AND BOWLS
Pudding basins come in a range of sizes and are made of tough porcelain which won't crack even in the pressure cooker. The steep tapered sides help the pudding keep its shape when turned out.

Stainless steel bowls are ideal for small jobs like melting chocolate over hot water, whisking egg whites and whipping cream. A *copper bowl* is only used for whisking egg whites and may be worth buying—they are expensive—if you make a lot of meringues, but the bowl requires special care.

MOULDS
Moulds have sloping sides which help to make turning out jellies and mousses easier than if the dish had straight sides. Moulds for foods which are chilled or frozen are best made of thin metal which helps speed up chilling time.

A *charlotte mould* is a large

A selection of pudding basins, bowls and moulds

A selection of baking dishes and flan, tart and pie tins

STEAMED PUDDINGS

Grease the pudding basin and put a round of greased greaseproof paper in the base. Fill not more than two-thirds full with the pudding mixture to allow room for expansion during cooking. Cut a piece of double greaseproof paper or foil to cover the basin and grease well. Make a pleat in the paper or foil in order to allow the pudding to rise.

Cover the basin tightly with the paper or foil and secure with string. If any moisture or water gets into the pudding it will sag or even collapse when turned out.

Place the basin in a large pan filled with boiling water to come halfway up the sides of the basin. Keep the water boiling rapidly all the time during steaming and have a kettle of boiling water on hand to top it up regularly. If you are using a saucepan and not a steamer the basin should be placed on a trivet—an upturned saucer or crossed skewers can be used—to keep the basin off the bottom of the pan. Keep the water gently bubbling so basin just wobbles.

To turn out a steamed pudding: Loosen the pudding at one side to let in some air, then invert it on to a warmed serving plate.

TO REHEAT A STEAMED PUDDING
Wrap the pudding in foil and heat through in a 180°C (350°F) mark 4 oven for 15–20 minutes.

TO COOK IN A PRESSURE COOKER
For a 1 litre (2 pint) pudding basin, pour about 850 ml (1½ pints) water into the bottom of the pressure cooker. Stand the pudding on a trivet and steam without pressure for 15 minutes, then bring to L (low) pressure and cook for about 2 hours depending on the pudding. Release pressure slowly.

round mould with sloping sides and is used for making the classic charlotte russe. *Decorative moulds* can make jellies and mousses look especially attractive. These moulds come in tall, flat, funnelled or tubular shapes. Individual-sized decorative moulds are also available. *Bombe moulds* are curved and come with a lid. *China moulds* are used for blancmange and other cornflour-thickened puddings as metal can sometimes tinge the colour of a milk-based pudding.

How long a pudding takes to set in a mould largely depends on its size. If using individual-sized moulds instead of one large mould setting times can be shortened by as much as 2 hours.

To prepare a mould for a chilled dessert rinse it under cold running water and keep the wetted mould in the refrigerator until the mixture is ready for it.

BAKING DISHES
A *soufflé dish* has straight sides to allow the greatest height when the soufflé mixture rises in the oven. It can be made of porcelain, earthenware or glass and comes in a range of sizes. Soufflé dishes are also useful for making mousses and baked custards. Individual-sized soufflé dishes are often used for baking instead of *ramekins*, which are slope-sided dishes used for crème caramel. Little *custard pots* are used for making *petits pots de chocolats*.

A *spring-release tin* has a side section which can be removed without disturbing the base. These often come with alternative bases. Cheesecakes are usually baked or chilled in these tins.

FLAN, TART AND PIE TINS
Flan rings can be fluted or plain and are about 2-cm (1-inch) deep; they come in a range of sizes. Use flan rings together with a baking sheet or baking tray—make sure the baking sheet lies flat and has not buckled.

Flan tins can double as sandwich tins; some have levers to ease unmoulding. Other flan tins are fluted and many come with a removable base. These are primarily used for pastry flan cases. For *sponge flans* use a special flan tin with a raised base.

Ceramic *pie dishes* are usually used for baked fruit pies. They have a wide rim for preparing the pastry edge of a single crust pie. *Pie plates* are shallow, round dishes made of metal, ovenglass or earthenware; they are used for the traditional single crust 'plate pie'.

Individual tarts are made in sheets of *tartlet moulds* or in individual moulds.

Cooking with Fruit

Fruits can make desserts and puddings so varied and delicious. Each fruit offers its own distinctive flavour and texture that it is worth trying as many types as possible when they are in season to make simple fruit salads or creamy mousses and sorbets. Dried fruit and nuts extend the choice even further, while the use of sweeteners and the addition of gelatine offer the opportunity of creating many more delicious sweet dishes.

GLOSSARY OF FRESH FRUIT

APPLES

Apples are available all year round and are at their best in the late autumn months. Cooking apples tend to be larger than eating apples. They are too tart to eat on their own but when cooked with sugar they have a wonderful sweet and sharp flavour. Cooking apples are juicy and will cook to a fluffy purée. When making purées add the sugar towards the end of cooking time. To help apples keep their shape add the sugar at the start of cooking. Look for Bramley's Seedling, Lord Derby and Grenadier.

Eating apples often have more flavour than cooking apples. Cox's Orange Pippin, Newton Wonder, Laxton Superb, Worcester Pearmain and Granny Smith all have distinctive flavours, making them good additions to raw fruit salads and to pies, tarts and puddings. These apples also hold their shape more easily during cooking. Avoid mealy tasteless apples. Less sugar is needed when cooking eating apples.

Look for firm apples with unblemished skins. Keep apples cool and dry. Apples kept at room temperature should be eaten within 2 weeks. Simply wipe and wash before eating.

To prepare them for cooking, apples are usually peeled and then quartered and cored. An apple corer is a handy gadget which

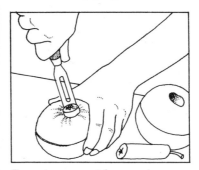
Removing cores with an apple corer

makes coring easy and neat. Apple slices should be brushed with lemon juice to prevent browning.

APRICOTS

Unripe apricots are hard and sour; overripe ones will be mealy and tasteless. Leave apricots to ripen at room temperature. Once ripe, they should be eaten within 2–3 days. Apricots are available for a relatively short period in spring and summer.

Cracking apricot kernels

Prepare apricots by washing, cutting them in half and removing the stone. To peel apricots, blanch in boiling water for 30 seconds to loosen the skins, then peel. Sliced apricots should be brushed with lemon juice to prevent browning. Apricot stones have a subtle almond flavour. Crack the kernels and use to flavour sugar syrups when poaching apricots.

BANANAS

Bananas for eating are picked hard and green. When buying look for evenly coloured skins. They are ready to eat when yellow and slightly flecked brown. They will ripen if kept in the dark at room temperature. Once peeled bananas should be brushed with lemon juice to prevent discolouring.

BLACKBERRIES

Blackberries ripen in late summer and early autumn. When buying avoid stained containers as this may indicate crushed fruit below. Once picked blackberries lose their flavour rapidly and if bought should be eaten on the same day.

To prepare blackberries, wash them and remove the stalks. Remove any damaged fruit. Blackberries are especially good cooked with other fruit such as apples. They can be baked, bottled, eaten raw or frozen. Freeze only fully ripe undamaged fruit, without washing. Damaged or wet fruit can be cooked before freezing but will only keep for about 6 months.

CHERRIES
Cherries are a summer fruit. A number of different types are available as the different varieties have a very short picking time. Cherries are sold mainly on the stalk. Avoid split, diseased or immature fruit. For raw eating cherries look for large soft berries either white, red or black. Smaller hard varieties are better for cooking.

Prepare cherries by rinsing them in a colander and removing the stalks. Cherry stoners are available for the purpose or you can cut into them with the point of a knife and prise out the stone.

Stringing currants with a fork

CURRANTS
Currants are ripe in midsummer. Blackcurrants are more common than red or white. They are normally on a strip or stalk and are more expensive when not. Avoid withered or dusty currants; choose firm ones with a distinct gloss. To remove the currants from their stalks use a fork to rake them off. Currants can be frozen raw, cooked or pulped. If storing in the refrigerator keep covered for up to 10 days, removing damaged fruit.

DAMSONS
Damsons are available in September to early October. Select ripe but firm fruit showing no bird or insect damage. Store them in a cool place and cook soon after purchase as ripe damsons do not keep. Prepare damsons by washing and halving them. The

Halving damsons with a knife

stones can be taken out with a sharp knife. Damsons need to be cooked with a sweetener as they are very sour. They are best frozen in sugar syrup but the skin will toughen.

GOOSEBERRIES
Unripe gooseberries are always green. As they ripen they turn gold, red or even white; some of them bear whiskers. Buy evenly coloured fruit, keep it refrigerated and eat within 3 days. Wash the gooseberries and snip off the stem and flower ends (top and tail); discard damaged fruit. Gooseberries are sour and will always need sweetening. For puddings, slightly immature fruits are better.

Snipping off gooseberry stems

Ripe gooseberries do not freeze well but barely or under ripe fruit can be frozen. Cooked gooseberries stewed or pulped will keep frozen for up to 1 year.

GRAPEFRUIT
These large citrus fruits are always available. Select evenly coloured glossy fruit. They will keep for 4 days at room temperature and 2 weeks refrigerated.

Prepare grapefruit by cutting in half and separating the flesh from the skin with a serrated knife. Then divide the segments. Or, peel the skin off cutting just below the pith, then hold the fruit in one

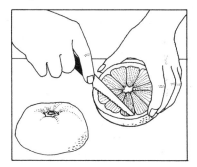

Segmenting with a serrated knife

hand and cut out the segments with the other leaving the protective membrane behind.

GRAPES
Grapes can range from pale amber to a deep blue colour. Buy plump unbruised grapes still attached to their stems. Keep grapes refrigerated and use within 3 days. Grapes should be left unwashed until ready to serve. Pips can be removed by halving the fruit with a knife and flicking out the pips with a knife. To leave the fruit whole, push a sterilised hair pin into the grape and push out the pips. Remove the skins by placing grapes in boiling water for 20 seconds; the skins can then be peeled off with a knife. Black grapes are not usually peeled.

KIWI FRUIT
(Chinese gooseberries)

Available from midsummer to late winter, kiwi fruit are egg shaped with a brown furry skin. Ripeness is tested by gentle pressure and a slight yielding of the flesh. Kiwi fruit should be kept at room temperature until ripe and then used within 2 days. Preparation simply consists of peeling the fruit with a small sharp knife and slicing the bright green flesh crossways. There is a pleasant pattern of edible black seeds in the flesh.

KUMQUATS

Kumquats are very small members of the orange family, about the size of a plum. They are available all the year round. They should have smooth shiny skins; avoid those with shrivelled skins. They can be stored at room temperature for up to 2 days and refrigerated for up to 1 week. Prepare kumquats by rinsing them (in a colander) and removing the stems. Halve lengthways or leave whole, and slice thinly for dessert decoration. Both the skin and flesh are eaten and they are best when poached.

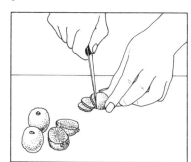

Slicing kumquats thinly

LEMONS AND LIMES

Lemons and limes are available all year round, though limes are not sold as widely as lemons. Limes are greener than lemons (the darker the colour the better) and slightly smaller but for preparation limes may be treated the same way as lemons. Look for lemons which are a strong 'lemon yellow'

colour and have a moist-looking skin; they should feel heavy for their size. A shrivelled skin will indicate that some of the juice has evaporated. Lemons will be at their best for only a few days if kept at room temperature and up to 2 weeks in the refrigerator.

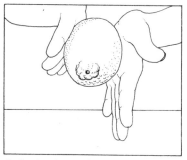

Softening lemon for maximum juice

To extract the maximum amount of juice from a lemon or lime, it should be at room temperature. Roll the fruit back and forth in your hands, pressing gently with the palm to help soften the fruit. Then slice the fruit in half crossways and either squeeze hard or use a lemon squeezer. *One large lemon contains about 30 ml (2 tbsp) juice.*

The skins of limes are tougher and much thinner than those of lemons and so release much less zest. When grating lemon zest make sure that none of the bitter tasting white pith is grated. To thinly pare lemons, peel the rind with a vegetable peeler, again avoiding any of the bitter white pith.

LOGANBERRIES AND TAYBERRIES

Both these fruits can be treated the same as raspberries and are available in the summer months. They do not keep well. Very ripe fruit should be eaten right away. Only freeze dry fruit which is just ripe. For eating raw, make sure the fruits are firm, dry and fully ripe. Second-quality fruit can be puréed and frozen.

MANGOES

Mangoes are available most of the year except in early winter. Ripe mangoes are very juicy and have a yellow or orange skin; they should give to a gentle squeeze. Avoid soft or shrivelled mangoes. Ripe mangoes should be kept and used within 3 days.

To prepare mangoes, cut a large slice from one side of the fruit, cutting close to the stone. Cut another slice from the opposite side. The flesh in the cut segments can be scooped out into squares lengthways and crossways without breaking the skin. Push the skin inside out to expose the cubes of flesh. Use a sharp knife to peel the remaining centre section and cut the flesh away from the stone in chunks or slices.

MELONS

Melons are available all year round except for watermelons which are only available in summer, the time of year when melons are most abundantly available. Depending on the variety, melons can be smooth skinned or have a light or heavy netting. Many have a light or heavy ridging—conveniently the ridges can be used as guides for serving portions. Ogen, charentais and galias are round melons and can be small or large. Honeydews are usually large round shapes or they can be oval. All melons have a highly perfumed sweet juicy flesh. Usually, the more fragrant the melon the sweeter and juicier its flesh will be.

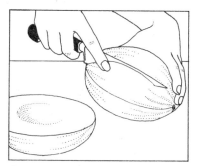

Cutting melon into wedges

Melons should be stored tightly wrapped in the refrigerator as they can easily pick up the flavours of other foods. Ripe melons are firm but have a slight give when pressed at the ends. Use within 2–3 days. Soft patches on the rind indicate bruising rather than ripeness. Buy slices or wedges only if they have been kept with the cut surface covered with cling film.

TO SERVE ROUND MELONS

Cut melons in half crossways and scoop out the seeds with a spoon. They will look more attractive if the edges are cut in a zig-zag pattern. To use the halves as *melon bowls*, cut a small slice off the bottom of each half so they stand upright. Keep the bowls tightly wrapped in the refrigerator until ready to serve.

TO MAKE MELON WEDGES

Halve fruit lengthways, scoop out seeds and cut into wedges. Cut the flesh free from the rind, but leave in place; divide it into cubes.

TO MAKE MELON BALLS

Scoop out the melon flesh with a melon baller.

NECTARINES

Nectarines can be bought from midsummer to early autumn and from early winter into the spring. Shop for plump rich-coloured fruit softening along the indent. Hard, extremely soft or shrivelled fruit should be avoided. Nectarines will ripen at room temperature but once ripened should be refrigerated and used within a period of 5 days.

Preparation is simply washing. They may be peeled with a sharp knife if desired then halved and stoned. Brush the exposed flesh with lemon juice to stop discolouring.

ORANGES

Oranges are at their best in the early months of the year. Choose firm fruit that feel heavy and have a glossy skin. Avoid those with dry or hard looking skins. Thick-skinned navel oranges are easy to peel and are seedless; thinner-skinned oranges are more difficult to peel but are usually more juicy and have a more pronounced orange flavour.

Oranges will keep for 4 days at room temperature and if wrapped

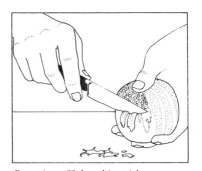

Scraping off the white pith

and stored in the refrigerator they will keep for at least 2 weeks.

When serving sliced oranges the white pith should be scraped off with a knife after the orange is peeled. When dividing the oranges into segments hold the fruit over a bowl to catch all the juices. The pith is more easily removed from warm oranges than cold ones. Pour over boiling water to cover and leave the oranges for several minutes before peeling.

To use orange peel in cooking, peel the rind with a vegetable peeler avoiding any of the bitter white pith, then blanch the peel for 3 minutes, rinse under cold water and then shred before using.

PEACHES

Peaches are available all the year round, but are at their best in summer. Ripe peaches are slightly soft and have a yellow to orange skin. Avoid green, bruised or 'sale' fruit. Eat peaches within 2 days if kept at room temperature or if wrapped and chilled within 5 days. Peaches can be peeled by immersing them in boiling water for about 15 seconds, then cooking in cold water. Use a sharp knife to separate the loosened skin from the flesh. Very ripe peaches are best if skinned and stoned under running water, as scalding them will soften and slightly discolour the flesh. Cut lengthways along the indentation in the fruit and twist the fruit in half, then remove the stone. Brush cut fruit with lemon juice to prevent browning.

TO MAKE A MELON BASKET

Honeydews and watermelons can be used to make large baskets and small round melons such as ogens can be used to make individual baskets. Cut a thin slice off the bottom of the melon so it will stand upright. Make 2 cuts each about 1 cm (½ inch) from the top stem of the melon and cut straight down to the centre of the melon.

Then slice horizontally to make 2 wedges; remove the wedges. Remove the seeds from the centre of the melon and evenly cut away the flesh from the piece that is forming the basket handle. Scoop out the melon flesh with a large spoon or melon baller, discarding seeds if using a watermelon. Chill, tightly wrapped, until required.

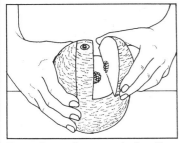

Removing wedges to make handle

Scooping out flesh with a spoon

UNUSUAL FRUIT

The variety of fruits available seems to be ever increasing as we see more and more unusual looking fruits in markets bearing prickly wrinkled skins, odd shapes and often giving off exotically perfumed aromas. These fruits are often very expensive but can be bought in very small quantities and used to liven up fruit salads or to make unusual decorations for puddings. In a moment of extravagance they can be used to make very special sorbets. Many of them are available canned. Preparing them need not be a mystery.

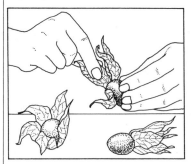

Bending calyx on cape gooseberries

Cape gooseberry or Chinese lantern. When ripe the berries are enclosed in a lantern-shaped case or calyx, and are orange yellow in colour. If the case or calyx is bent back to form a petal around the central berry, they can be used as a decoration for cakes. They can also be eaten raw or added to fruit salads.

Custard apples. The flesh has a flavour reminiscent of custard and is soft and pulpy in texture. Cut the fruit in half and scoop out the flesh with a spoon.

Dates. The stones of fresh dates can be easily removed by cutting off the stem end and gently squeezing the date—the stone should slip out. Fresh dates are plump with a slightly mealy texture. Slice and add to fruit salads.

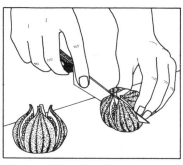

Slicing and opening figs for serving

Figs. These can be simply sliced or partially sliced and opened like a flower. They are juicy and have a more delicate flavour than their more frequently used dried counterpart.

Guavas. A juicy fruit full of seeds, guavas can be pear-shaped, or round looking like tomatoes. They should be peeled then puréed or baked.

Breaking and peeling lychee skin

Lychees. The hard, red-brown scaly skin should be broken and then peeled. The white pulpy flesh surrounds a soft brown stone. Remove the stone and serve the lychees chilled. They have a distinctive flavour—slightly acid yet sweet.

Papaya. A large smooth-skinned fruit which ripens from green to yellow to orange. Slice the fruit in half and remove the black seeds in the centre. Cut into slices and add to fruit salads—papayas have a smooth soft texture and a distinctive rich flavour.

Passion fruit. Most varieties we see have a hard brown wrinkled skin. Slice the fruit in half and scoop out the flesh with a teaspoon; the seeds can be eaten and when passion fruit is used in fruit creams and sorbets the seeds should be included in the purée.

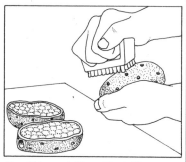

Scrubbing prickles off prickly pear

Prickly pear or Indian Fig. A prickly pear has a greenish-orange skin covered with tiny prickles. The sweet juicy pink flesh has edible seeds. Wash and scrub off the prickles, cut off each end, slit downwards and peel back the skin. Slice the flesh and serve with a squeeze of lemon juice.

Halving sharon fruit with a knife

Sharon fruit or persimmon. The most frequently found variety of persimmon in this country is the sharon fruit. It looks like a large plump tomato and has a sweet, slightly sour tasting flesh. Unlike other persimmons it is seedless and both skin and flesh are eaten. The flesh can be puréed and used in many types of ice-creams and mousses.

PEARS

Pears are available all the year round. Buy well formed firm pears with no oozing or softness. Ripe pears give a little at the stem end. They do not remain ripe for long and so should be checked often. They will ripen indoors but then should be refrigerated and used within 3 days. For eating raw, Williams, Conference, Comice or Lacton's are good. Use firm pears for cooking.

Prepare pears by washing and peeling; scoop out the core with a teaspoon. A pear wedger will core

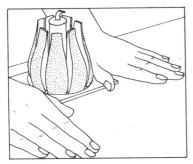

Slicing and coring with a wedger

and cut a pear quickly. Lemon juice will prevent slow deterioration of peeled pears.

PINEAPPLES

Pineapples are available all year round. Ripe pineapples give off a sweet aroma and in addition a leaf will pull easily from the crown. Avoid pineapples that are bruised or discoloured or have wilting leaves. These fruits continue to ripen after picking and are often sold slightly unripe. However a really unripe pineapple with no aroma will not ripen properly. The most common method of preparation is to cut off the leaf crown and cut the pineapple into thick slices crossways. Use the tip of the blade to trim off the outer skin and remove the tiny brown spots from the flesh. Use either a small knife or an apple corer to remove the central core. Pineapples can also be served in wedges. Cut the fruit in half and

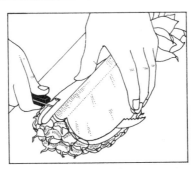

Separating pineapple flesh

then quarters lengthways, cutting through but not removing the leaf crown. Use a small knife to cut out the exposed central core. Use a curved knife to separate the flesh from the skin and cut it downwards in order to make wedge-shaped slices.

PLUMS

The different varieties of this fruit are available from the late spring to early autumn. The colour may vary from yellow or green to red or almost black. Hard, shrivelled or split plums should be avoided. Sweet plums can be eaten raw and all varieties can be cooked. Sweet or dessert plums will ripen at home in a few days. Greengages are sweet, amber-coloured plums; deep purple Victorias are good all-rounders.

Prepare plums by washing and halving them. Stones can be removed with the tip of a knife.

Plums freeze well, preferably top-quality just ripe fruit. The stones if left in during the cooking will produce an almond–like flavour. Some varieties of plum skin hardens in freezing. If freezing in sugar syrup add ascorbic acid or lemon juice.

POMEGRANATES

Pomegranates are available in the autumn. Buy fruit with hard russet coloured skin. Keep pomegranates refrigerated and use within 7 days. Prepare by cutting a slice off the stem end with a sharp knife. Then slice the skin sections lengthways and draw the sections

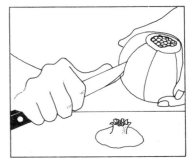

Slicing pomegranate skin

apart. Push in the skin and push out the seeds from the inside. Seeds can be eaten or juiced. Pomegranates should not be frozen.

QUINCES

Quinces are available in October to November. Avoid scabby, split or small fruit. The apple-shaped quinces stew well and the pear-shaped ones keep well. Store them in a cool dry place away from absorbent foods likely to be affected by the strong aroma of quinces. A few quinces are eaten raw but most are cooked with other fruit, especially apples. To prepare quinces simply peel and slice or chop.

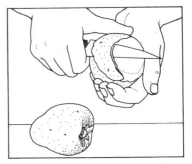

Peeling quinces with a sharp knife

RASPBERRIES

The main season for raspberries is from late June to mid August although some varieties are sold into early autumn. Raspberries are sold hulled which makes them liable to crushing. When shopping avoid stained containers and wet fruit especially. After damp weather they are likely to mould quickly; any deteriorating fruit should be discarded as soon as possible. Use only the best dry fruit at the point of ripening when freezing. Over-ripe or damaged fruit may be sieved and frozen as pulp.

RHUBARB

Forced rhubarb can be bought in winter and early spring; maincrop rhubarb comes in spring and early summer. Forced rhubarb is pink and tender looking and sweet tasting. Maincrop variety has a stronger colour and a thicker stem and is more acid to taste. Rhubarb should be kept cool or refrigerated and used within 4 days. If maincrop rhubarb looks a little limp it can be stood, leaf up, in cold water, like flowers, to crispen. To prepare rhubarb, chop off and discard the leaves and root ends and wash the stems. Some maincrop rhubarbs have a tougher stem which may need peeling. Chop the

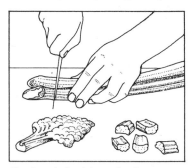

Cutting rhubarb into chunks

stems into chunks for cooking. For short term freezing trim the ends, wash, drain and freeze. For longer freezing blanch it in boiling water for 1 minute.

SATSUMAS AND TANGERINES

Look for these fruits in the winter months. Choose small loose-skinned varieties with a bright orange colour. Avoid dry ones or those with patches of soft skin. They will keep at room temperature for a few days or if kept

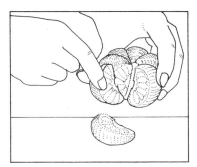

Segmenting satsumas/tangerines

refrigerated up to 10 days. The skin does not cling to the flesh and can be peeled off by hand. Pick off remaining bits of white pith. Divide the fruit into segments, eat raw or in salads.

STRAWBERRIES

A true summer fruit, the majority available during the summer season are British grown. As with most berries check the base of the punnet for staining as this will indicate squashed fruit. Strawberries are probably most famous for being eaten raw, with cream but are also delicious puréed and chilled. Be sure to buy plump glossy berries with their green frills still attached. Only wash berries just before hulling. Sugared, hulled strawberries yield the juice readily. Besides eating raw strawberries can be stewed and put into flans, tarts and pies. Freeze only the best just ripe fruit. Damaged or over-ripe fruit can be frozen as pulp with a little lemon juice or citric acid added.

Puréeing strawberries with a sieve

FRUIT SAUCES

The distinctive flavours of fruit sauces will add enormously to the enjoyment of desserts and puddings. Because fruit sauces are often sharp and tangy as well as quite sweet, they can be the perfect complement to bland desserts such as meringues, cold soufflés, pancakes or simple steamed puddings and they come into their own when simply poured over vanilla ice-cream.

Fruit sauces are very simple to make. Usually a purée of fruit is sweetened and lightly thickened. *Cornflour* is always first dissolved in a cold liquid before it is added to a hot one, otherwise it will be lumpy. Cornflour thickened sauces need to be cooked to remove the raw taste of the starch; during this time the sauce thickens. A sauce thickened with *arrowroot* will be clear and shiny but it should be served soon after making as arrowroot soon loses its thickening properties.

FRUIT SAUCE

Makes 300 ml ($\frac{1}{2}$ pint)

425 g (15 oz) can fruit in syrup
10 ml (2 tsp) arrowroot or cornflour
squeeze of lemon juice (optional)

1 Strain the juice from the fruit. Sieve the fruit, make up to 300 ml ($\frac{1}{2}$ pint) with juice and heat until boiling.

2 Blend the arrowroot with a little of the unused fruit juice until it is a smooth cream and stir in the puréed fruit. Return the mixture to the pan and heat gently, continuing to stir, until the sauce thickens and clears. Stir in the lemon juice if using.

——— VARIATION ———

Omit the lemon juice. Add 15 ml (1 tbsp) rum, sherry or fruit liqueur to the sauce immediately before serving.

BILBERRY SAUCE

Makes 600 ml (1 pint)

450 g (1 lb) bilberries, washed
225 ml (8 fl oz) water
15 ml (1 tbsp) cornflour
175 g (6 oz) caster sugar
pinch of salt
5 ml (1 tsp) lemon juice

1 Trim the bilberries. Bring the water to the boil, add the berries and bring back to the boil.

2 Meanwhile, mix the cornflour to a smooth paste with a little cold water. Stir it into the bilberries with the sugar and salt and cook until the mixture has thickened, stirring constantly, then add the lemon juice.

GOOSEBERRY SAUCE

Makes 400 ml (¾ pint)

225 g (8 oz) gooseberries, washed
50 g (2 oz) sugar
300 ml (½ pint) water
juice of 1 orange
15 ml (1 tbsp) cornflour

1 Trim the gooseberries. Put the sugar and water into a large saucepan and heat gently until the sugar has completely dissolved. Add the gooseberries and simmer until they are tender.

2 Mix the orange juice with the cornflour, stir in a little of the gooseberry juice and pour the mixture into the sauce, stirring well. Bring to the boil and simmer for 1–2 minutes until the sauce has thickened.

CREAMY PLUM SAUCE

Makes 400 ml (¾ pint)

4 eating plums, washed
100 g (4 oz) icing sugar
225 g (8 oz) cream cheese, softened

1 Halve and stone the plums. Put them in a blender with the sugar and blend until smooth, or rub through sieve to remove skins.

2 Add the cream cheese and beat until well blended. Cover and chill until required.

BRANDIED CHERRY SAUCE

Makes 400 ml (¾ pint)

450 g (1 lb) cherries, washed and stoned
100 ml (4 fl oz) brandy
100 g (4 oz) sugar
10 ml (2 tsp) cornflour
5 ml (1 tsp) almond flavouring

Put the cherries into a large saucepan with the brandy, sugar and cornflour and cook, stirring all the time, until the mixture has thickened and just begins to boil. Remove from the heat and stir in the almond essence.

MELBA SAUCE

Makes 400 ml (¾ pint)

450 g (1 lb) raspberries
60 ml (4 tbsp) redcurrant jelly
15 ml (1 tbsp) icing sugar
30 ml (2 tbsp) arrowroot
15 ml (1 tbsp) water

1 Rub the raspberries through a sieve into a saucepan. Add the jelly and sugar and bring to boil.

2 Blend the arrowroot with the cold water to a smooth cream and stir in a little of the raspberry mixture. Return the sauce to the pan and bring to the boil, stirring with a wooden spoon, until it thickens and clears. Strain and leave to cool.

FRUIT PURÉES

Many fruit sauces are based on purées. Usually the fruit is first cooked with sugar until softened. Soft berry fruits however are sometimes not cooked before puréeing. The softened fruit is rubbed through a sieve which should be nylon as metal can sometimes react with the acid in the fruit and taint the flavour. Although it is much simpler to purée the fruit in a blender or food processor it may still be necessary to sieve the fruit in order to remove any small pips. A fruit purée can make a simple dessert on its own served with cream.

FRUIT GLAZES

Glazes not only give fruit flans and tarts a shiny covering but they also help protect the fruits from discolouring or drying out.

When making fruit glazes use a jam which complements the colour of the fruit to be covered. About 150 ml (¼ pint) glaze is enough to cover two 20-cm (8-inch) flans.

APRICOT GLAZE

Makes 150 ml (¼ pint)

100 g (4 oz) apricot jam
30 ml (2 tbsp) water

Glazing a fruit flan

Sieve the jam into a small saucepan and add the water. Heat gently, stirring, until the jam softens. Bring to the boil and simmer for 1 minute. Allow to cool until warm then spoon over the flan or tart.

——— VARIATION ———

Redcurrant Use redcurrant jelly instead of apricot jam; there is no need to sieve the jelly, just stir until completely blended.

DRIED FRUIT

Dried fruits add a concentrated natural sweetness to a number of puddings. Keep them in the store cupboard as a useful standby for making winter fruit salads and fruit compotes.

Although dried fruit is most frequently bought in small packages, large packages of raisins and sultanas are a more economical buy as are dried fruits sold loose or in bulk from some health food shops. Packaged dried fruits are always pre-washed but fruit sold loose should be washed.

Store dried fruit in a cool, dark place. Unopened packages will keep for up to 1 year. Once opened or if bought loose, store the fruit in an airtight tin. For best flavour use within 3 months.

To make interesting fruit salads select from the more unusual variety of dried fruits like *pears*, *peaches*, *apples* and *bananas*. Dried bananas look like elongated figs and should not be confused with the sweetened banana chips which are usually eaten as a snack food. Dried *apricots* have a more pronounced and usually better flavour than their fresh counterpart and when reconstituted can be used to make flans, tarts and pies in the same way as fresh apricots.

For making attractive cake decorations choose from the large variety of candied fruits. These fruits which are preserved in sugar syrup can have a glossy coating in which case they are known as *glacé fruits* or they will have a granulated coating when they are known as *crystallised fruits*. Candied fruits are widely available at Christmas time when they are served as a luxurious sweetmeat. Leftovers can be chopped and used to decorate puddings.

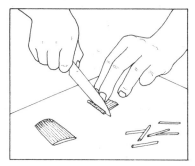

Cutting angelica into strips

TO MAKE ANGELICA LEAVES

Cut the angelica into 0.5-cm ($\frac{1}{4}$-inch) strips, then cut each strip into diagonal slices.

Angelica is the traditional decoration for fruit trifles. Look for angelica with a good green colour. Large pieces of *candied peel*, or 'caps', are preferable to the ready-chopped peel. Freshly cut candied peel will have more aroma and flavour. Peel can be cut into slivers and used to decorate cold soufflés and mousses, in an attractive border. *Crystallised violets and roses* can also be used for decorating puddings. Buy them in small quantities and store them in a cool, dark place to avoid bleaching. *Glacé cherries* are used whole or sliced for decorating; they come in red, green and gold colours.

Store all candied fruits in a cool, dry place and use within 6 months.

TO CLEAN DRIED FRUIT

Wash the fruit, removing any stalks or leaves, and spread them out over muslin or absorbent kitchen paper on a wire rack. Leave them to dry for 2–3 hours. Alternatively, to quickly clean the fruit, rub the fruit on a wire sieve or in a tea towel with a little flour, then pick over to remove any stalk. Do not dry fruit over direct heat as this tends to make them hard.

TO PLUMP DRIED FRUIT

Sultanas and raisins can become hard during storage and currants are naturally hard. These fruits can be plumped in a little hot water or some of the recipe liquid for about 30 minutes before using. Soaking them in sherry or brandy will add extra flavour.

TO SOAK DRIED FRUIT

Other dried fruits should be soaked for at least 3 hours or even overnight. Soak the fruit in cold water, but to shorten the soaking time pour over boiling water to cover and leave the fruits to soak. Prunes will taste better if soaked in cold tea or red wine. Dried fruit doubles its weight when soaked. No-need-to-soak apricots and prunes are available and these require no preparation.

Soaking prunes in cold tea

TO CHOP DRIED FRUIT

Dried fruit can be chopped in the same way as nuts. They can also be snipped with scissors. To prevent the fruits from sticking, lightly flour them or use icing sugar. Sugar-rolled chopped dates are available.

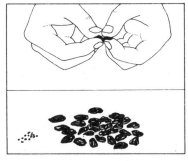

Removing pips from raisins

TO STONE RAISINS

Most raisins that we buy are seedless. Stoned raisins, however, are large, juicy raisins with an excellent flavour. These raisins become misshapen and stick together in a mass but are well worth separating and using. They should be checked before using to ensure that all the pips have been removed. Large dessert raisins sold loose in specialist shops also need to have the pips removed if they are to be used in cooking. Work the raisins between the fingertips to remove the pips, occasionally dipping the fingers in warm water.

TO STEW DRIED FRUIT
Cook them in the soaking water adding 100–175 g (4–6 oz) sugar and a small piece of lemon rind to every 600 ml (1 pint) water. Stew gently until soft and serve hot or cold with custard sauce.

TO REMOVE THE SUGARY COATING FROM GLACÉ FRUITS
The glossy coating on cherries and other glacéd fruits should be removed before they are used in baking, otherwise the fruit will sink to the bottom of the pan as it is dragged down by the sugary coating. Rinse the fruit under warm running water and pat dry with absorbent kitchen paper.

Tossing glacé cherries in flour

Toss the fruit in a little of the recipe flour before adding to the pudding or cake mixture. Glacé fruits used to decorate desserts will lose their lustre if washed, but the sugary coating also tends to seep on the topping if they are applied much in advance of serving.

NUTS

The more that nuts have been prepared by the producer the more convenient they will be to use, but they will usually be more expensive than the whole nuts. Nuts prepared at home will also have more flavour because they will have had less chance to dry out and lose their aromatic properties. Ready-shelled nuts are much more convenient to have on hand than whole nuts. Do not use flavoured or salted nuts in desserts.

Buying nuts in bulk can be economical but the high fat content in nuts means that they can become rancid, especially walnuts, pecans and peanuts. Ideally nuts should be used within 1 month and kept stored in a cool place in an airtight tin. To extend their shelf life, nuts can be very successfully frozen and usually can be used from frozen without thawing. Old nuts can be crisped in the oven before using.

Of all the nuts used in dessert making none is more versatile than *almonds* with their sweet distinctive flavour. They are sold whole in their skins, blanched, split, flaked and ground. Almonds are widely used to make decorations on gateaux and creamy puddings. *Praline* is a combination of sugar and almonds which is crushed to make a dessert topping or it can be folded into ice-cream mixtures and meringues. *Hazel nuts* are another popular dessert-making nut. Besides being used finely chopped for dessert toppings they are also folded into meringues and ice creams. Hazel nuts can also be used to make praline. Whole, chopped and ground hazel nuts are available. *Brazil nuts* are usually eaten as a sweetmeat, sometimes dipped in chocolate, but the large nut can also be flaked by using a vegetable peeler and then toasted and used as a decoration. Finely-chopped *walnuts* added to crumb crusts gives them a fuller, richer flavour and walnuts are a welcome addition to hot sauces for ice creams and puddings. Walnuts can be successfully substituted for the more expensive *pecans*, a nut with a very soft texture and rich mild flavour. *Cashews, peanuts pistachio nuts* and *macadamia nuts* all can be used to add interesting variations to puddings and dessert decorations; use coarsely chopped and sprinkled over cold desserts.

TO BLANCH NUTS
Nuts are blanched by being boiled briefly and then skinned. Place almonds in a pan of cold water, bring just to the boil, then strain and run under cold water. The skin can be easily slipped off be-

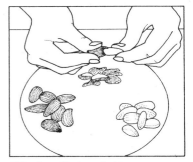

Slipping off almond skins

tween the thumb and finger. Freshly blanched almonds are more easily chopped, or flaked. Pistachio nuts should be boiled for about 3 minutes.

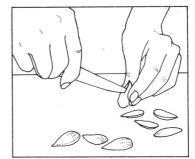

Splitting almonds with a knife

TO SPLIT ALMONDS
Almonds can be split by inserting the tip of a very sharp knife between the two halves of the nut and separating them.

TO SKIN HAZEL NUTS AND PEANUTS

The thin inner covering of shelled nuts is usually peeled because it has a bitter taste. Heat through the nuts in the oven or toast under a low grill. Tip the hot nuts into a clean cloth and rub until the papery skins slip off.

TO TOAST AND ROAST NUTS

The flavour of nuts is often more pronounced if they are first toasted. Pale-coloured almonds turn a golden colour making them especially attractive for dessert decorations. Spread whole, chopped or slivered nuts on a baking tray and toast them under a medium grill, turning the nuts occasionally, until they have darkened. Alternatively, they can be roasted in a 180°C (350°F) mark 4 oven for 10–12 minutes. Nuts can also be dry fried in a frying pan for about 5 minutes. Watch nuts carefully as they can suddenly burn.

TO CHOP NUTS

Nuts can be simply chopped on a board using a long, sharp knife.

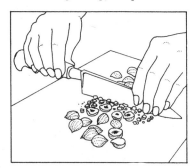

Chopping nuts on a board

Gather the nuts into a pile against the flat of a knife and slice firmly through the nuts, with the knife held against your finger. Steady the tip of the blade with your hand and chop rapidly. Keep collecting the nuts into a pile and repeat chopping until chopped to the desired size. Walnuts and pecans are soft-textured nuts and may be more easily chopped by snipping them with scissors.

Because of the shape and hard texture of hazel nuts they are more easily chopped in a very clean coffee grinder. A food processor can also be used for chopping nuts but care must be taken when using these machines that the nuts do not grind to a flour or paste.

TO GRIND NUTS

Nuts ground at home will have more flavour and aroma than bought ones. Almonds and hazel nuts are often used ground, especially almonds for making marzipan. Ground nuts are good to sprinkle over a flan case before filling with a juicy fruit filling — they help to absorb the fruit juices and ensure the baked blind crust remains crisp as well as adding extra flavour.

Grind nuts in a coffee grinder or food processor. Grind for about 1 minute turning the grinder on and off frequently during grinding. Only grind a little at a time. Be careful that the nuts do not turn to a paste.

PRALINE

Makes about 100 g (4 oz)

75 g (3 oz) granulated sugar

25 g (1 oz) blanched almonds, chopped and toasted

1 Oil a baking sheet. Place the sugar with 60 ml (4 tbsp) water in a saucepan and heat gently, stirring all the time, until the sugar dissolves. Bring to the boil and boil steadily, without stirring, until golden brown.

2 Add the almonds and pour at once on to the prepared baking sheet. Leave to set for about 10 minutes.

3 Crush the praline finely with a rolling pin or in a food processor or blender.

COCONUTS

To prepare a coconut, puncture the shell at the eyes with a screw-

driver and hammer. Drain off the milk into a jug or bowl. Store, covered, in the refrigerator for up to 2 days. (Use to make drinks.) Crack the shell by hitting the widest part of the coconut all around with a hammer or the back of a cleaver.

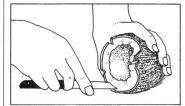

Separate the halves and prise the flesh from the shell with a small sharp knife.

TO SHRED AND TOAST COCONUT

Using a sharp knife remove the rough brown skin and shred the white flesh on a coarse grater or grate in a food processor or blender. Freshly grated coconut can be toasted in a 180°C (350°F) mark 4 oven until golden brown.

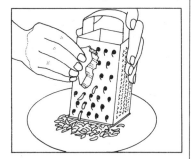

Stir the coconut frequently. Store up to 4 days.

Desiccated coconut, a dried unsweetened coconut, and *shredded coconut*, a sweetened coconut, are also available.

SUGAR

Desserts depend on sugars for their sweetening power, and they also give many desserts their characteristic textures and consistencies as well as colour — the smooth syrupy consistency of many sauces, the soft spongy texture of gateaux, the crispness of meringues and the rich colour of some steamed puddings. When using sugar be careful about altering the amount called for in the recipe: too little sugar or too much and the texture of your dessert may be spoiled. Remember sugar tastes much sweeter when desserts are served hot — so less sugar is needed. Conversely, cold puddings require more sugar and will taste almost too sweet before they have cooled.

Granulated sugar is the all-purpose sugar. More care is needed when using it to make desserts as its coarse crystals can easily cause textures to be gritty or granular if not properly dissolved. Granular sugar is used for making sugar syrups. Relatively new is *natural granulated sugar* which retains some of the sugar's natural brown colour. It can be used as ordinary granulated sugar, except where colour is important.

Caster sugar is most frequently used in dessert making. Although more expensive than granulated sugar its fine crystals readily dissolve when beaten with eggs or heated. Caster sugar can be made at home by grinding granulated sugar in a blender or food processor. Good to have on hand is *Lump sugar* which is not only used for sweetening hot drinks but is good to use when making lemon or orange flavoured desserts: the lumps of sugar can be rubbed on the rind of citrus fruits to extract the zest, thereby giving the dessert a more pronounced citrus flavour.

The powdery fine texture of *icing sugar* makes it ideal for using with uncooked fruit purées which are used for making sorbets or sauces — it quickly dissolves without heat. Icing sugar is used for making icings and also makes a simple and attractive topping when lightly sieved over cakes, pies and pastries. Do not use it for baking as the volume produced will be dense and heavy.

Brown sugars can be either fully refined white sugars which have been tossed in molasses to give them colour and flavour, or they can be partially refined sugars which retain some of their natural brown colour; these natural brown sugars are called Barbados sugar, Muscovado sugar or molasses sugar. They tend to be moister than other brown sugars but their cooking properties are the same.

All brown sugars, natural or artificial, light or dark, cream easily with butter. Unlike white sugar brown sugar not only sweetens but adds flavour as well, especially dark brown sugar which adds a treacle like flavour and dark colour to many steamed dried fruit puddings and fruit cakes. *Demerara sugar* is a moist sugar with large crystals; it is usually used as a crunchy topping for puddings.

Liquid sweeteners
The special flavour of *golden syrup* combines particularly well with spices. It is less sweet than granulated sugar and so is usually used in combination with other sugars, but it comes into its own when used as a dessert topping. *Honey* also makes a lovely dessert topping. It absorbs and retains moisture and helps prevent cakes from drying out and going stale. Only part of the sugar content should be replaced by honey — usually not more than half — otherwise the texture will be altered. When honey is used to make ice-creams they will have a softer consistency.

Black treacle and molasses add dark colour and a distinctive, flavour to steamed puddings.

TO MEASURE GOLDEN SYRUP AND HONEY

To measure with a measuring spoon, first warm spoon under hot water — scooping the sweetener will be easier, *25 g (1 oz) golden syrup or similar sweetener is equal to 15 ml (1 tbsp).*

Measuring with a warm spoon

SUGAR SYRUPS

Sugar syrups form the basis of a number of simple fruit desserts and they are also used when making bottled fruits and for freezing fruits. Sugar syrups vary in the amount of sugar which is dissolved in water: they can be light, medium or heavy. Which one you make depends on the intended use or on the type of fruit.

Although these syrups are boiled they are only boiled for 1 minute — quite unlike the lengthy boiling and bubbling up of syrups made for use in confectionery.

When making a simple sugar syrup the sugar must first be slowly dissolved over gentle heat before it is brought to the boil, otherwise when cooled the syrup may crystallise. The sugar is then boiled for 1 minute. To cut the time for the syrup to cool dissolve the sugar in half the water, bring the water to the boil for 1 minute, then add the remaining water. If the syrup is to be used while still boiling, keep the lid on the pan to prevent evaporation, which would alter the strength of the syrup. *To make a light sugar syrup use 225 g (8 oz) granulated sugar for every 600 ml (1 pint) water.* This syrup is used when making fresh fruit salads, for poaching fruits and in freezing fruits like fresh dates and figs, slices of lemon and lime and rhubarb and pineapple.

To make a medium sugar syrup use 350 g (12 oz) granulated sugar for every 600 ml (1 pint) water. This syrup is used for soaking savarins and rum babas and for freezing fruit like apples and oranges and stoned fruits.

To make heavy sugar syrup use 450 g (1 lb) sugar for every 600 ml (1 pint) water. Use for bottling and freezing fruit such as most tart soft berry fruits.

POACHED OR STEWED FRUITS IN SUGAR SYRUP

Fresh fruits lightly cooked in a flavoured sugar syrup make a simple yet elegant dessert, especially when served with cream or

Turning fruit during poaching

custard. Use firm fruits as soft fruits will not hold their shape easily. When cooking fruits use a heavy-based pan large enough for the fruit to stand in one layer so that it cooks evenly. Turn the fruit occasionally with a slotted spoon. *For every 450 g (1 lb) fruit use 600 ml (1 pint) light sugar syrup.* The fruit should be very gently simmered in the sugar syrup until it is almost cooked—usually this takes about 5–7 minutes. To prevent the fruit from becoming mushy remove the pan from the heat and leave the fruit in the pan, covered, for several more minutes while it finishes cooking.

FLAVOURINGS FOR 450 g (1 lb) POACHED FRUIT

Apples Add a squeeze of lemon juice, a strip of lemon rind, 1 or 2 cloves or a small piece of cinnamon stick.
Peaches Add 45–60 ml (3–4 tbsp) brandy after the fruit has cooked.
Pears Add 1 or 2 cloves or a piece of cinnamon stick.
Plums Add the plum kernels or a few sweet almonds.
Rhubarb Add a piece of bruised root ginger, a piece of cinnamon stick or, alternatively, a strip of lemon or orange rind.

CARAMEL SUGAR

To make caramel sugar, granulated sugar is cooked until it turns a brown colour. The caramel can range from straw-coloured to a deep brown; this depends on how long the sugar is cooked. Caramel sugar tastes much less sweet than ordinary sugar and has a distinctive flavour.

To make a hard caramel, the browned sugar is poured on to a lightly oiled baking tray and left until brittle and hard. It can then be broken into pieces or crushed to a powder with a rolling pin. Use sprinkled on puddings in the same way as praline.

Caramel sugar can also be thinned with water to make a syrup for crème caramel or caramelised oranges. Be very careful when adding water to the hot

Sprinkling pieces of hard caramel

sugar—it will spurt and bubble. Remove the pan from the heat and add the water very slowly. If the syrup is too thin, it can be boiled until reduced to the desired thickness. A caramel syrup can also be made by first dissolving the sugar in the water over low heat and then boiling until the syrup turns the desired shade of brown.

TO COAT A DISH WITH CARAMEL

The dish to be coated with caramel should be warmed to enable the caramel to slide more easily over it. If using a metal dish, wear oven gloves or hold the dish in a cloth as the hot caramel quickly heats the dish. Tilt the

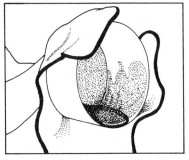

Coating a dish with caramel

dish gently until it is evenly coated. Allow the caramel to cool slightly before adding custard.

FLAVOURED SUGARS

Bay leaf Store caster sugar with 1–2 bay leaves in a tightly closed airtight tin. Use the sugar for making milk puddings.
Lemon or orange Mix 100 g (4 oz) caster sugar with the finely grated rind of 1 lemon or orange. Leave the sugar to dry then store in a tightly covered airtight tin.
Vanilla Store 1 whole vanilla pod in a tightly closed airtight tin of caster sugar.

GELATINE

Gelatine is a tasteless substance which when chilled gives fruit and milk jellies and mousses their special wobbly and soothing consistency.

Powdered gelatine is sold loose in cartons or in measured envelopes, each containing exactly 11 g (0.4 oz) gelatine which is the equivalent of 15 ml (1 tbsp). This amount of gelatine will set 500 ml (1 pint) of liquid. If too much gelatine is used the finished dessert will be stiff or rubbery. However, sometimes about 5–10 ml (1–2 tbsp) extra gelatine is added if the gelatine is to be served during hot weather or if the mixture is very acidic. To use powdered gelatine, always add the gelatine to the liquid. Place a small amount of cold recipe liquid in a heatproof cup or bowl and sprinkle in the gelatine. Stand the bowl over a saucepan of hot water and heat gently until the gelatine has dissolved. Use 45 ml (3 tbsp) recipe liquid for each 15 ml (1 tbsp) powdered gelatine. The gelatine must not be allowed to boil as boiling prevents proper setting from taking place.

Leaf gelatine is a more expensive alternative to powdered gelatine; it comes in sheets of transparent gelatine. It is reputed to give a clearer set and less likely to cause lumps. Four sheets of leaf gelatine is equivalent to 15 ml (1 tbsp) powdered gelatine and will set 500 ml (1 pint) liquid. It needs to be soaked in about 45 ml (3 tbsp) recipe liquid per 4 sheets for about 10 minutes. Snip the gelatine into small pieces with scissors before soaking. The soaked gelatine can then be dissolved in the same way as for powdered gelatine.

When making *fruit jellies* warm the required amount of liquid, sweeten and flavour it, then quickly stir in the dissolved gelatine. The more closely the two are

the same temperature the more easily the gelatine can be evenly blended with the liquid.

To hasten the set, heat one-half of the liquid, add the gelatine then combine with the remaining cold liquid. Jellies will also set more quickly if the mixture is put into small moulds or individual containers. If using a proprietary jelly tablet, use half the hot water, making up the remainder with ice cubes; as the ice melts the jelly cools and sets.

For mousses and other cold mixtures a little of the cold mixture should be added to the hot dissolved gelatine, then, holding the bowl high above the mixture pour it in a thin steady stream on to the cold mixture, whisking all the time so that the gelatine is completely blended.

Chilling takes up to 4 hours but longer if it contains fruit. For a firm set allow 12 hours.

TO UNMOULD A JELLY OR MOUSSE

Draw the tip of a knife or your finger around the rim of the mould to loosen the edge of the jelly. Immerse the mould in hot water for 2–3 seconds and place a

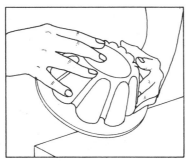

Unmoulding jelly onto a plate

wetted serving plate on top of the mould. Hold in position with both hands then quickly invert together giving one or two sharp shakes. If the mould is not positioned in the centre, the wetted plate will make moving it into position easier.

TO SET FRUIT IN JELLY

Fresh pineapple juice, pineapple

and kiwi fruit contain an enzyme which breaks down gelatine and destroys its setting powers. Boil pineapple juice for 2–3 minutes to kill the enzyme. Do not use fresh or frozen pineapple or kiwi fruit.

Prepare a variety of fresh fruits such as black grapes, bananas, sections of oranges and raspberries. Pour about 2.5 cm (1 inch) clear lemon jelly into a mould and arrange a little of the fruit in this. Allow the jelly to set. Add more jelly and fruit and allow to set. Continue until mould is filled.

ORANGE JELLY

Serves 2–3

300 ml (½ pint) cold water
20 ml (4 tsp) powdered gelatine
75 g (3 oz) lump sugar
1 lemon
3 oranges

1 Place 45 ml (3 tbsp) water in a small bowl and sprinkle in gelatine. Stand bowl over a pan of hot water and heat gently until dissolved. Cool slightly.

2 Rub the lump sugar on the rind of the lemon and 1 of the oranges to extract the zest, then add sugar to remaining water. Heat gently until sugar is dissolved. Stir in gelatine.

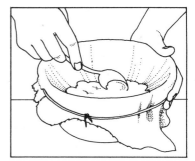

3 Squeeze the juice from the fruit and strain it. Add water to make up to 150 ml (¼ pint) and add to the gelatine mixture. Strain through muslin into wetted mould. Cool, then chill until set.

Cooking with Chocolate and Cream

Chocolate and cream are probably the most popular and versatile of dessert ingredients— whether used as part of the dessert itself or as an attractive and mouth-watering finishing touch. Use them separately or, for extra richness, together. They come in many forms, however— make sure you choose the right one for your needs.

CHOCOLATE

In order for a chocolate product to be labelled chocolate it must have a legal minimum of 34 per cent cocoa solids.

Cocoa powder is often used in gâteaux and puddings. As it is unsweetened, sugar must be added in order for it to be palatable.

Cooking chocolate costs no more than plain chocolate. It is often sold loose in delicatessens broken in large pieces, or in a bar which is marked in measured segments.

Chocolate-flavoured cake covering has very good melting qualities and is used for icings and for making moulded sweets, but because it lacks the true chocolatey flavour it should not be used unless called for in the recipe.

Plain chocolate has varying amounts of sugar and may be labelled *bitter* or *semi-sweet* depending on its sugar content.

TO MELT CHOCOLATE
Chocolate can suddenly burn and so needs to be very gently melted. Break into small pieces and place them in the top of a double saucepan over hot, but not boiling, water. Leave until melted. Be sure to keep both water and steam away from the melting chocolate, as the chocolate can become grainy and lose its smooth appearance if moisture gets into it.
　　Chocolate can also be melted in a 110°C (225°F) mark $\frac{1}{4}$ oven. Place the pieces in an ovenproof bowl and leave until melted. If you melt the chocolate over direct heat, use a heavy-based saucepan and stir constantly with a wooden spoon to prevent the chocolate burning. When adding chocolate to hot liquids like custards and milk, remove the hot liquid from the heat and stir in pieces of chocolate to evenly blend.
　　If melted chocolate thickens or

curdles because it has become too hot add a little blended white vegetable fat. Break fat into small pieces and stir into mixture until it reaches desired consistency.

DECORATING WITH CHOCOLATE
Chocolate decorations make desserts look more appetising, and they add a little extra flavour. Use chocolate to decorate coffee, orange, strawberry, mint and vanilla-flavoured puddings. There are a number of ways to decorate with chocolate. Whichever way it is used, handle the chocolate as little as possible. Body heat melts chocolate and leaves fingerprints on the surface. Use a hard (plain) chocolate for chopping and grating; a soft chocolate like milk chocolate can be used to make curls and shapes.
　　Simple chocolate decorations can consist of chocolate *sugar strands* (vermicelli) or crumbled *chocolate flake* sprinkled over a pudding. Plain chocolate can be grated by peeling off flakes or

Grating with a vegetable peeler

curls from the edge of a bar of chocolate with a swivel-bladed vegetable peeler. It is wise to keep the chocolate being grated in its wrapper except for the surface being grated to help prevent the chocolate melting.
　　For more interesting decorations pour melted chocolate on to a cool marble slab or baking tray, making a thin layer. Leave it to cool until it loses its tackiness and make either of the following:

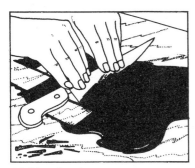

Making chocolate caraque

Caraque Use a long sharp knife and hold the blade in both hands. Push or draw the knife sideways across the surface of the chocolate making curls. By adjusting the angle at which the knife is held you will vary the size of the curls.

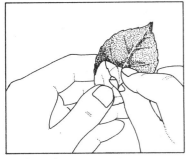

Making chocolate rose leaves

Leaves Using a knife, thinly spread melted chocolate on the undersides of clean, dry, un-damaged rose leaves. Leave to set. Gently peel leaf off chocolate.

Stamping out chocolate shapes

Shapes Cut the chocolate into neat triangles or squares with a sharp knife or use petits fours cutters to stamp out other shapes.

CREAMS

Creams vary in their fat content which is why some creams are richer than others. In order for cream to whip it must have a fat content of at least 35 per cent.

Half cream and *single cream* will not whip. They are ideal pouring creams for puddings and fruits.

Soured products *Soured cream* gets its thick spoonable texture from a bacterial culture added to single cream. *To make soured cream: add 15 ml (1 tbsp) lemon juice to 150 ml (5 fl oz) single cream.* *Yogurt* is also made with a bacteria culture but is made from milk. *Greek yogurt* made from ewe's milk and imported from Greece and *Greek-style yogurt*, made from cow's milk, have an especially creamy, thick texture, but also a higher fat content than other yogurts. All make a delicious alternative to cream as a topping for fruit pies and desserts.

Spooning cream and *'extra-thick' double cream* have been homogenised to make them thick and spoonable. *Clotted cream* has a slightly nutty flavour and thick consistency. These creams will not whip but are excellent for serving with pudding or fruit. *UHT creams* will keep for months. UHT cream only whips to a light foam.

Whipping cream will whip to at least double its volume; *double cream* will whip to slightly less volume than whipping cream, but *adding 15 ml (1 tbsp) milk for every 150 ml (5 fl oz) double cream will help it to achieve a greater volume.* Both are good for piping decor-ations and cake fillings; whipping cream is especially good for folding into mousses. Both can be cooked without risk of curdling, unlike single cream, half cream, or soured cream. Whipped cream with added vanilla flavouring and sugar makes *Chantilly cream*.

ICE CREAMS AND SORBETS

The knack of successfully making creamy smooth ice creams and sorbets largely involves making sure that no large ice crystals form during freezing. When making ice creams and sorbets without special

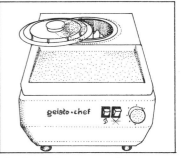

An electric ice cream maker

equipment it is necessary to periodically whisk the freezing mixture until smooth. Electric ice cream makers and *sorbetières* can be put directly into home freezers. (An electric cord passes through the rubber seal and should be used according to manufacturers' instructions.)

When making ice cream and sorbets the freezer should be turned to fast freeze or to its lowest setting because the quicker the mixture freezes the less likely the risk of crystallisation. Sorbets are usually made with a sweetened fruit purée or juice. It must be highly flavoured and sweetened as freezing diminishes sweetness and flavour. Too much sugar and the mixture will not freeze properly; too little sugar and the mixture turns to a block of ice. Some sorbets are made with the addition of whisked egg whites which are folded into the mixture once it has partially frozen. This helps prevent large ice crystals forming.

Transfer ice creams and sorbets from the freezer to the refrigerator at least 30 minutes before serving to soften. Ice cream can be stored in the freezer for up to 3 months. Sorbets are best eaten within 1 month of making as they gradually develop ice crystals.

Cooking with Eggs

Eggs are invaluable for making desserts. They make soufflés and mousses light and produce the creamy smooth texture of custards, sauces and ice creams. But eggs are temperamental and special care is needed when using them to ensure success every time. Eggs have an added bonus — they are a hidden nutrient in seemingly indulgent desserts.

Egg whites become foamy by trapping air when whisked; this special property enables them to act as a raising agent for batters and cakes, either alone or in combination with the yolk. When whisked separately egg whites give soufflés and meringues their characteristic lightness. The coagulating or thickening property of egg yolks is what makes thick custards and sauces when heat is applied.

Eggs need to be cooked gently and slowly, otherwise they will become too tough.

Buy the freshest eggs possible. All egg boxes give the week number in which the eggs were packed, weeks running from Monday to Saturday and numbered beginning with 1 for the week in which January 1 falls. Avoid buying eggs that are stored near a sunny window or radiator in the shop. Eggs are graded according to weight; size 4 is the size most frequently used in dessert recipes.

A fresh egg broken on to a flat surface will have an upstanding yolk and the whites adhering to it. Old eggs will have thin runny whites. To test for freshness put the egg into a tumbler of cold water. If the egg is fresh it will lie flat at the bottom of the glass. If

Testing an egg for freshness

the egg tilts slightly it is starting to become old and if it floats it is very likely to be bad.

TO SEPARATE AN EGG
Give the egg a sharp knock against the side of a basin or cup and

Breaking egg shell on basin edge

break the shell in half; tapping the egg several times may cause it to crack in several places and not break evenly. Pass the yolk back and forth from one-half of the shell to the other letting the white drop into the basin.

When separating more than one egg it is a good idea to use a third bowl for cracking the eggs as a precaution against a yolk breaking and spoiling the whites. Put the second yolk in with the first one and tip the white in with the first white. Continue using the third bowl in this way.

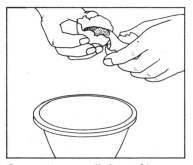

Separating egg yolk from white

EGG WHITES
When egg whites are whisked tiny globules of air are trapped in the egg to form an almost tasteless substance, which when added to other ingredients gives them an airy and light texture. If heat is applied to the egg whites the trapped air expands further

causing the mixture to rise further as in soufflés. Whisked egg whites also can become firm and hard without losing their shape, as in meringues.

Egg whites will achieve maximum volume when whisked in a metal bowl; copper is best but stainless steel is also good. Use a balloon whisk as a rotary or electric beater cannot be circulated as well throughout the eggs.

Eggs that are 2–3 days old will whisk to a greater volume than new laid eggs. For best results separate the eggs 24 hours before using them and store them in a covered container in the refrigerator. An acid such as cream of tartar added to the eggs or rubbing the bowl with lemon helps whites hold their shape when whisked.

What is important is that the bowl and the whisk are immaculately clean. If egg whites come into contact with any grease or dirt they will not whisk to maximum volume. Any egg yolk present in the whites and volume also decreases plus the eggs will take much longer to foam. Salt also adversely affects the foaming of egg whites.

Start whisking with a slow circular movement and gradually work faster, lifting the eggs high out of the bowl to help incorporate as much air as possible. Whisk until the egg whites stand in stiff,

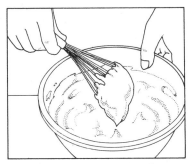

Whisking egg whites until stiff

pointed peaks when lifted from the eggs. Stiffly beaten egg whites should not fall out of the bowl if the bowl is upturned.

If using an electric beater, start on the lowest speed and gradually increase the speed. If the eggs are beaten too much the foam becomes dry and brittle and other ingredients such as sugar will not easily be incorporated.

FOLDING IN EGG WHITES

Mixtures combine more easily when their consistency and temperatures are similar. Folding in is best done with a metal spoon or plastic spatula. Use a continuous

Folding in with a metal spoon

cutting and lifting movement, scooping right down to the bottom of the bowl. Scoop one way turning the bowl the other. Stop folding as soon as the mixture is blended. Too much folding and the egg white may start to liquify.

Use leftover egg whites for glazing pies, pastry and breads. Mix lightly with a pinch of salt and brush over rolls and breads.

● Use egg whites to make meringues or soufflés.

● Egg whites and egg shells are used for clarifying stocks and for making clear jellies.

● Add a stiffly whisked egg white to whipped cream to make a lighter texture and to stretch the cream.

● A lightly beaten egg white is used for coating when deep-frying.

● Egg whites will keep in the refrigerator for 3–4 days. Cover tightly.

CUSTARD SAUCE
Makes 300 ml (½ pint)

2 eggs
10 ml (2 tsp) caster sugar
300 ml (½ pint) milk
5 ml (1 tsp) vanilla flavouring (optional)

1 Beat the eggs with the sugar and 45 ml (3 tbsp) milk. Heat the rest of the milk until warm and pour it slowly on to the eggs, beating all the time.

2 Pour into a double saucepan or bowl standing over a pan of simmering water. Cook, stirring constantly, until the custard thickens enough to coat the back of a spoon.

3 Pour into a chilled jug and stir in the vanilla flavouring. Serve warm or cold. The sauce thickens on cooling.

CRÈME PÂTISSIÈRE (Confectioner's custard)
Makes 300 ml (½ pint)

2 eggs
50 g (2 oz) caster sugar
30 ml (2 tbsp) plain flour
30 ml (2 tbsp) cornflour
300 ml (½ pint) milk
vanilla flavouring

1 Cream the eggs and sugar together until thick and pale in colour. Sift and beat in the flour and cornflour and a little cold milk to make a smooth paste.

2 Heat the rest of the milk in a saucepan and stir over low heat until the mixture boils. Add a few drops of vanilla flavouring to taste and cook for a further 2–3 minutes until thick and smooth. Cover and leave until cold before using as required.

MERINGUES

The light, crisp texture of meringues is the perfect foil to creamy fillings and slices of soft fruit. Meringues are made with whisked egg whites to which sugar is incorporated. They are very slowly baked in the oven in order to dry out and become crisp and firm. They are a perfect way to use up leftover egg whites because meringues will keep in an airtight tin for as long as 6 weeks.

There are three basic types of meringue although for home cooking only meringue Suisse is usually made. Meringue *cuite* and Italian meringue are both made by cooking the egg whites and this enables the meringue to be stored if necessary before shaping. These meringues are harder, whiter and more powdery than meringue Suisse but require more painstaking care and extra muscle power for whisking.

Meringue Suisse is made by incorporating sugar into stiffly beaten egg whites. Caster sugar or a combination of caster and granulated sugars are used. First one half of the sugar is very gradually added, about 15 ml (1 tbsp) at a time, while whisking after each addition until the sugar is fully incorporated and partially dissolved. Sugar added in large amounts at this stage may result in a cooked meringue which is sticky. The remaining sugar is added by sprinkling it over the whisked whites and folding it in with a metal spoon. The egg whites should be firm and glossy.

Meringue topping is made in the same way as meringue Suisse except that the amount of sugar is slightly decreased. Instead of using 50 g (2 oz) per 1 egg white, 40 g (1½ oz) per egg white is used. The meringue is spread over the filling, which should be warm to help the meringue stick to it. It is baked at a higher temperature than other meringues to make its characteristic light spongy texture.

MERINGUE SUISSE

Makes about 15 individual meringue shapes

3 egg whites, size 2

75 g (3 oz) granulated sugar and 75 g (3 oz) caster sugar or 175 g (6 oz) caster sugar

1 Grease a baking sheet or line it with aluminium foil or non-stick paper.

2 Whisk the egg whites until stiff. Gradually add 75 g (3 oz) granulated or caster sugar, whisking well after each addition. Fold in the remaining sugar very lightly with a metal spoon.

3 Spoon the meringue into a piping bag fitted with a large star nozzle and pipe small rounds on to the prepared baking sheet. Alternatively, spoon the mixture in small mounds on to the prepared baking sheet.

4 Bake in the oven at 130°C (250°F) mark ¼ for about 2½–3 hours, until firm and crisp, but still white. If they begin to brown, prop open the oven door a little. Remove the meringues from the baking sheet and leave until cold on a wire rack.

MERINGUE NESTS

Spoon the meringue into six mounds, spaced well apart on the prepared baking sheet; hollow out centres with the back of a spoon.

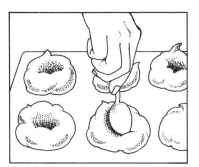

Hollowing out meringue nests

MERINGUE BASKET

Grease a 23-cm (9-inch) pie dish and spoon in the meringue. Pile the meringue high around the sides of the dish to make a basket.

MERINGUE FLAN CASE

Draw a 20.5-cm (8-inch) circle on a sheet of non-stick paper and place the paper mark side down on a baking sheet. Spread some of the meringue over the circle to form the base of the flan. Using a large star nozzle pipe the remainder to form the edge of the flan, or make a rim with the aid of a spoon. Bake for 1½–2 hours.

PAVLOVA

3 egg whites

175 g (6 oz) caster sugar

2.5 ml (½ tsp) vanilla flavouring

2.5 ml (½ tsp) distilled white wine vinegar

5 ml (1 tsp) cornflour

300 ml (½ pint) double cream

fresh strawberries, raspberries, kiwi fruit, or canned passion fruit, drained

1 Draw an 18-cm (7-inch) circle on non-stick paper and place the paper mark side down on a baking sheet.

2 Whisk the egg whites until very stiff. Whisk in half the sugar, the flavouring, vinegar and cornflour with a metal spoon.

3 Spread the meringue mixture over the circle and bake in the oven at 150°C (300°F) mark 2 for about 1 hour until crisp and dry. Leave to cool on the baking sheet then carefully remove the paper.

4 Whisk the cream until stiff. Slide the meringue on to a flat plate, pile the cream on it and arrange the fruit on top.

SOUFFLÉS

Hot soufflés are based either on a sweet white sauce to which egg yolks and flavourings are added, or on a crème pâtissière, in which the egg yolks are already incorporated. Cold soufflés are usually based on fruit purées.

HOT VANILLA SOUFFLÉ

Serves 4–6

50 g (2 oz) caster sugar
4 eggs, size 2
60 ml (4 tbsp) plain flour
300 ml (½ pint) milk
2.5 ml (½ tsp) vanilla flavouring
icing sugar (optional)

1 Butter an 18 cm, 1.7 litre (7 inch, 3 pint) soufflé dish. Cream the sugar with one whole egg and one yolk until pale cream in colour. Stir in the flour. Pour on the milk and mix until smooth.

2 Pour the mixture into a saucepan and bring to boiling point, stirring, and simmer for 2 minutes. Cool slightly. Beat in remaining yolks and flavouring.

3 Whisk the egg whites until stiff then fold into the mixture. Pour into the prepared soufflé dish and bake in the oven at 180°C (350°F) mark 4 for about 45 minutes until well risen, firm to the touch and pale golden. If you wish, after 30 minutes cooking, dust soufflé with icing sugar and continue to bake. Serve at once.

STRAWBERRY SOUFFLÉ

Serves 4–6

350 g (12 oz) strawberries
30 ml (2 tbsp) powdered gelatine
60 ml (4 tbsp) caster sugar
20 ml (4 tsp) lemon juice
3 egg whites
pinch of salt
200 ml (7 fl oz) double cream

1 Reserve six strawberries for decoration. Purée the remainder in a blender.

2 Put gelatine and 15 ml (1 tbsp) sugar in a saucepan, add one third of purée and stir over gentle heat until gelatine dissolves.

3 Remove from the heat, stir in the remaining purée and the lemon juice and pour into a bowl. Chill until the mixture mounds slightly when dropped from spoon.

4 Prepare a paper collar (see page 48) for a 600-ml (1-pint) soufflé dish. Place dish on a baking sheet for easier handling.

5 Whisk egg whites and salt until soft peaks form. Add remaining sugar a little at a time, whisking well, until stiff peaks form.

6 Beat the chilled strawberry mixture in a mixer until fluffy. Whip cream until soft peaks form and combine with strawberry mixture. Carefully fold in egg whites.

7 Spoon soufflé mixture into dish and smooth the top. Chill for 4 hours until set. Peel off the collar from dish. Decorate with reserved strawberries.

PANCAKES

Pancakes are made with a batter of pouring consistency. Most batters will improve if they are left to rest in a cool place for at least 30 minutes before using; this will help make a lighter pancake. If the pancake mixture thickens after resting it can be thinned with a little milk. Pancake batters made with a whisked egg white must be used straight away.

PANCAKES

Makes 8 pancakes

125 g (4 oz) plain flour
pinch of salt
1 egg
300 ml (½ pint) milk
lard

1 Mix the flour and salt together, make a well in the centre and break in the egg. Add half the liquid. Gradually work in the plain flour. Beat until smooth.

2 Add the remaining liquid gradually. Beat until the ingredients are well mixed.

3 Heat a little lard in a small frying pan running it around pan to coat sides. Raise handle side of pan slightly. Pour a little batter in from raised side.

4 Place over a moderate heat and cook until golden underneath, then turn with a palette knife and cook the other side. Slide the pancake on to a plate lined with greaseproof paper. Repeat.

Pastry Making

Good pastry making is a knack which comes only from practice and an understanding of the ingredients and how they are combined. There are a number of types of pastries, each with their own special uses. All are worth knowing how to make if you want your desserts to have that extra home-made taste. Shortcrust pastry being the most commonly used one is explained in detail on the following pages.

PASTRY

Flour, fat and liquid are the main ingredients of pastry. The method in which the fat is incorporated into the flour as well as the proportion of fat to flour determines the different types of pastry.

Shortcrust pastry is the most popular pastry. Not only is it quick and easy to make, but its firm texture makes it ideal for pies, flans and tarts. It uses half as much fat as flour. When making shortcrust pastry choose a fat which is firm at room temperature—it should be soft enough to rub yet firm enough so that the flour mixture does not mass into a lump. Butter gives the best flavour. Lard also gives a good flavour but is too soft at room termperature. For best results, use a combination of fats such as half lard and half white vegetable fat.

Flan or *rich shortcrust pastry* is a variation of shortcrust pastry, made with beaten egg instead of water and with sugar added if a sweet flavour is required.

With *puff pastry* and other flaked pastries the proportion of fat to flour is much higher than with shortcrust pastries. They are the richest of all pastries, rising in golden flaky layers.

Flaky pastry is less time consuming to make than puff pastry and is good to use when a rich pastry is required but the height of the pastry is not important. *Rough puff*, much the quickest to make, results in a less even or 'rough' texture. The light crisp texture and almost hollow centre of *choux pastry* is achieved by melting the fat (butter is used) and then quickly beating in the flour.

Strudel pastry or phyllo (filo) dough is a very crisp flaky pastry used for making strudels and Greek pastries. It must be made with strong plain flour to give the dough the elasticity it needs to be stretched until it is paper thin.

SHORTCRUST PASTRY

Good pastry making requires that you work quickly and handle the pastry as little as possible, otherwise the gluten in the flour will develop too much, resulting in an 'overworked' dough and tough pastry. With such a high proportion of fat it is important that work conditions be cool. Work on a cool surface; and always use your fingertips, which are cooler than your palms.

Rubbing in is the way that fat is incorporated into flour when making shortcrust pastries. The fat is cut into small pieces and rubbed into the flour in a bowl.

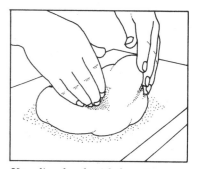

Kneading dough with fingertips

Kneading After liquid is added to the rubbed in mixture to bind it the dough should be gathered lightly together leaving the side of the bowl clean. Working on an unfloured surface, the dough is kneaded very lightly with the fingertips just long enough for it to be smooth and free from cracks.

Resting the dough Essential to all good pastry making is resting the dough to give the dough a chance to 'relax', making it easier to roll out and also to help prevent shrinkage during baking. Always tightly wrap the dough in cling film or foil or place it in a polythene bag to prevent a skin from forming and the pastry cracking. Refrigerate for 30 minutes. For shorter periods, rest dough under an upturned mixing bowl.

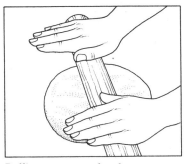

Rolling out pastry dough

Rolling out When rolling out pastry to the required shape and size never dust the pastry with flour. If necessary dust the working surface and rolling pin with as little flour as possible. With shortcrust pastry the dough can be rotated frequently to help create an even shape. Start by forming the dough roughly into the desired final shape and then roll away from you with short, quick rolls in one direction only. Rolled-out pastry should rest for 5 minutes before use.

SHAPING THE DOUGH

Avoid stretching the dough at any time otherwise it will only shrink when baked. It should also be handled as little as possible. Rolled out pastry can be transferred to the dish to be lined by placing the rolling pin at one end of pastry and very loosely rolling the pastry around it, then unrolling it over the dish to be lined or covered. Alternatively, it can be folded in half and placed on one half of the dish and opened out to cover the whole dish.

FREEZING

Pastry dough should be shaped before freezing as thawing can take over 3 hours. Unfilled pastry cases are very fragile. Foil plates or freezer proof ovenware should be used. Rounds of pastry can be stacked with waxed paper in between for pastry lids.

Open freeze pastry and wrap in foil; overwrap in polythene. Freeze for up to 6 months. Pastry

BAKING BLIND

When a pastry case is baked without a filling it is 'baked blind'. Having lined the tin or dish, cut a piece of greaseproof paper or foil to act as a lining. Place it in the pastry case and weigh it down with some dried beans, pasta, rice or ceramic baking beans. Bake pastry for 10–15 minutes, remove the weight and the lining and continue to cook the shell for a further 5 minutes. Allow the pastry time to shrink before removing it from its tin.

cases can be baked from frozen but allow about 5 extra minutes cooking time.

Freeze uncooked fruit pies for up to 3 months; cooked fruit pies will keep for 6 months.

Cook uncooked fruit pies from frozen in a 220° (425°) mark 7 oven for 40–60 minutes, according to type and size. Cooked pies should be thawed at room temperature for 2–4 hours, depending on type and size. Reheat, if necessary, in the oven.

QUANTITIES

Home-made pastry recipes indicate the amount of flour used to make the dough. A recipe calling for 350 g (12 oz) shortcrust pastry refers to the weight of the flour. As the portion of fat to flour in shortcrust pastry is half, this means you will need to make the pastry using 175 g (6 oz) fat. If you use bought shortcrust pastry, which is sold by total weight, you will need to buy a packet weighing at least one and a half times that of the flour weight called for in the recipe.

Pastry amounts given in recipes are usually very generous to allow for slight variations in tin sizes. However, leftover trimmings can be used to make decorations.

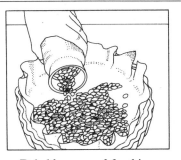

Dried beans used for this method may be used many times. Pastry cases so cooked will keep for a few days in an airtight tin and can be frozen.

FINISHING TOUCHES

Knocking up This is done after the edges have been trimmed and pressed together, both as a final seal and also to give a flaky appearance. While pressing the pastry with your index finger, tap the edge of the pastry with back edge of a knife held horizontally.
Fluting or Scalloping Use a round bladed knife or table knife. Make a series of curves around the pie with the inward points 1 cm ($\frac{1}{2}$ inch) inside the peaks of the flutes. Hold the pastry edge adjacent to where you are cutting.
Crimping With a thumb or finger of one hand push the pastry inwards gently. With the finger of the other hand pinch the pastry pushed up initially. Continue around the edge of the pie.

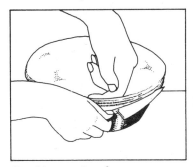

Knocking up edge of pastry

PASTRY DECORATIONS

Pastry decorations should be stuck to the pie by brushing them with water or a beaten egg before arranging them on the surface.

Making pastry tassels

Tassels Cut a strip from the rolled out pastry trimming 2.5 cm (1 inch) wide and 10–15 cm (4–6 inches) long. Cut 2-cm (¾-inch) slits at short intervals to resemble a fringe. Roll up and stand on the uncut end while you spread out the cut strips to form the tassel.

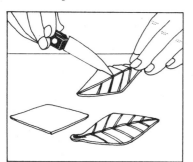

Marking veins on pastry leaves

Leaves Cut thinly rolled out pastry trimmings into 2.5-cm (1-inch) wide strips. Cut diagonally to diamond shapes and mark veins of a leaf on each one with back of a knife blade. Pinch one of long ends to form a stem.

Shapes Use petits fours cutters and small round cutters to make different pastry shapes. Cut out fruit shapes or letters to denote the type of fruit in the pie.

Glazes Pies can be glazed with milk or beaten egg. Apply any glaze just before baking otherwise pastry may be 'soggy'.

LINING A FLAN CASE

Choose a plain or fluted flan ring placed on a baking sheet or a loose-bottomed flan or sandwich tin, or a ceramic flan dish. Roll out the pastry thinly to a diameter approximately 5 cm (2 inches) wider all round than your ring or tin. Rolling your pastry around the rolling pin lift it on to the tin and then when centred unroll the pin from the pastry. By lifting the edges of the pastry it will settle into the shape of the ring or tin. Working away from the centre with your fingertips gently press the pastry into place, taking

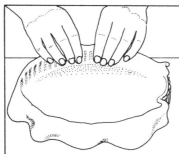

Fitting pastry into fluted tin

special care if it is fluted to ensure the pastry fits into all the 'flutes'. Make sure there are no air pockets between the pastry and the tin. You can now use a knife or scissors to trim the pastry or, if fluted, roll the excess pastry over the rim and run the rolling pin across the top for a neat trim.

A SINGLE CRUST PIE COVER

Roll out the pastry to a circle which is 7.5 cm (3 inches) wider than the tin or dish. Cut a 2.5-cm (1-inch) strip of pastry from around the edge which will leave 5 cm (2 inches) of pastry pro-

truding beyond the rim of the up-turned dish. Turning the dish right way up, brush the rim with water and lay the strip of pastry on to the rim and seal the join. Spoon the pie filling into the dish sufficient to make a slightly raised centre or place a pie funnel in the middle. Moisten the pastry rim and transfer the pastry lid on to the pie without stretching the pastry. Press the edge on to the pastry rim to make a seal. Trim the excess pastry with a knife held at an angle away from the dish. Knock up and pierce the lid to allow steam to escape. Excess pastry may be used to create decorative shapes on the top of the pastry lid.

LINING AND COVERING A DOUBLE PIE CRUST

Divide the dough into two, one part being slightly larger than the other. Shape both pieces into ball shapes ready for rolling. Start with the larger piece and roll it out until it is 2.5 cm (1 inch) wider than the rim of your pie plate. Transfer the pastry over the plate and allow it to settle into the shape. Taking care not to stretch the pastry, ease it to the shape of the plate making sure there are no air pockets. Put the pie filling, which should be cold, into the pastry-lined dish leaving a slightly raised contour in the middle. Roll out the smaller ball for the pie lid about 1 cm (½ inch) wider than the rim. Before transferring the lid onto the pie, brush the rim with water. Seal the edge, knock up and

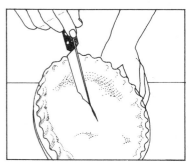

Making slit in centre of pie lid

glaze, making a short slit in centre of lid for the steam to escape.

LINING SINGLE AND DOUBLE TARTS

Roll out the pastry and use a cutter 2 cm (¾ inch) larger than the

Piling the filling into tarts

hollow in your tartlet tin. If lids are required, use a cutter the same diameter as the hollows. Press the larger rounds into the hollows of the tins. Pile filling into a heap in the centre of each tart. For a double tart brush the edges of the lids with water and place them wet side down over each tart. Press the edges of the lids on to the lower pastry linings to make a seal. Make a little incision in the top of each tart.

LINING SMALL MOULDS AND TINS

Arrange the tins to sit close together on a baking sheet. Roll out enough pastry to cover the area of tins. Transfer the pastry over the tins like a blanket. Twist off some of the pastry from around the edge and shape it into a ball

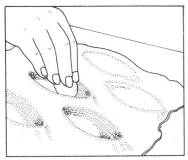

Easing pastry into small moulds

and lightly flour it. Use this knob to ease the pastry into each mould making sure there are no air pockets below the pastry. Use the rolling pin to remove the excess pastry by pressing it down and running it across the top of the moulds. Tidy the edges of the moulds with your fingertips and prick base and sides with a fork.

SHORTCRUST PASTRY

225 g (8 oz) plain flour
pinch of salt
50 g (2 oz) butter or block margarine
50 g (2 oz) lard

1 Sift the flour and salt together in a bowl. Cut the butter and lard into small pieces and add to the flour.

2 Lightly rub in the butter or margarine and the lard until the mixture resembles fine breadcrumbs.

3 Add 30–45 ml (2–3 tbsp) chilled water evenly over the surface and stir in until the mixture begins to stick together in large lumps.

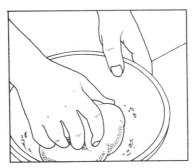

4 With one hand, collect the mixture together to form a ball. Knead lightly for a few seconds to give a firm, smooth dough. Do not over-handle.

5 The pastry can be used straight away, but it is better if allowed to 'rest' for about 30 minutes wrapped in foil in the refrigerator.

6 Roll out the pastry on a lightly floured surface to a thickness about 3 mm (⅛ inch). Do not pull or stretch the pastry. To cook, the usual oven temperature is 200–220°C (400–425°F) mark 6–7.

To freeze: Baked and unbaked shortcrust pastry freeze well. Thaw unrolled dough at room temperature before unwrapping; rolled out pastry may be cooked from frozen, allowing extra time.

SPONGE FLAN CASE

This is not strictly a pastry, but it is used in the same way as a convenient case for cold fruit mixtures.

melted lard for greasing
10 ml (2 tsp) and 50 g (2 oz) caster sugar
5 ml (1 tsp) and 50 g (2 oz) plain flour
2 eggs, size 2

1 Brush the inside of a 20.5-cm (8-inch) raised based flan tin with melted lard. Leave until set then sprinkle over 10 ml (2 tsp) caster sugar and tilt the tin to coat evenly. Add 5 ml (1 tsp) plain flour and coat similarly, knocking out any excess.

2 Place the eggs and 50 g (2 oz) caster sugar in a deep bowl and whisk vigorously, using an electric beater until the mixture is very thick. Sift 50 g (2 oz) flour over the surface of the mixture. Fold gently through with a metal spoon, then turn into the prepared tin and tilt to level the surface.

3 Place on a baking sheet and bake in the oven at 180°C (350°F) mark 4 for 20–25 minutes. When cooked, the sponge will have shrunk away from the edges of the tin, be a light golden brown and will spring back when pressed lightly. Ease away from the edges of the sponge with the fingers and turn carefully on to a wire rack. Leave for 30 minutes until cool.

Sweet Sauces and Butters

Sweet-flavoured sauces and butters are quick and easy to make, and are an excellent way of livening up a dessert. Try them as accompaniments to steamed and baked puddings, cold sweet soufflés and meringue desserts. Alternatively, sweet sauces are delicious simply poured over ice cream or fresh fruit.

SWEET BUTTERS

BRANDY BUTTER

Makes 6–8 servings

100 g (4 oz) butter, softened
100 g (4 oz) icing sugar, sifted
100 g (4 oz) caster sugar
15 ml (1 tbsp) milk
15 ml (1 tbsp) brandy

1 Beat the butter until pale and light. Gradually beat in the icing and caster sugars, alternately with the milk and brandy. Continue beating until light and fluffy. Pile into a small dish and leave to harden before serving.

--- VARIATIONS ---

Rum Butter Use soft brown sugar instead of caster sugar, replace the brandy by 45 ml (3 tbsp) rum and add the grated rind of $\frac{1}{2}$ a lemon and a squeeze of lemon juice.

Lemon or Orange Butter Omit the milk and brandy and add the grated rind and juice of 1 lemon or a small orange.

CHOCOLATE NUT BUTTER

100 g (4 oz) butter
10 ml (2 tsp) caster sugar
15 ml (1 tbsp) grated chocolate
30 ml (2 tbsp) chopped walnuts

1 Beat the butter until light and fluffy, then beat in the remaining ingredients.

SWEET SAUCES

SWEET WHITE SAUCE

25 ml (1$\frac{1}{2}$ tbsp) cornflour
300 ml ($\frac{1}{2}$ pint) milk
25 ml (1$\frac{1}{2}$ tbsp) sugar

1 Blend the cornflour with 15–30 ml (1–2 tbsp) of the milk to a smooth paste.

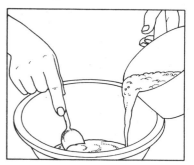

2 Heat the remaining milk until boiling and add to mixture, stirring. Return to pan and bring to the boil, stirring. Cook for 1–2 minutes after the mixture has thickened to a glossy sauce. Add sugar to taste.

--- VARIATIONS ---

When adding extra liquid to the sauce make a thicker sauce by increasing the quantity of cornflour to 30 ml (2 tbsp).

Flavour with any of the following when sauce has thickened:
5 ml (1 tsp) mixed spice
30 ml (2 tbsp) jam
grated rind of $\frac{1}{2}$ an orange or lemon
30 ml (2 tbsp) single cream
15–30 ml (1–2 tbsp) rum
1 egg yolk (reheat but do not boil)

CHOCOLATE SAUCE

Makes about 300 ml ($\frac{1}{2}$ pint)

175 g (6 oz) plain chocolate in pieces
large knob of butter
45 ml (3 tbsp) milk
45 ml (3 tbsp) golden syrup

1 Put the chocolate in a small bowl with the butter. Add the milk and syrup.

2 Stand the bowl over a pan of warm water and heat gently, stirring, until the chocolate has melted and the sauce is warm.

FUDGE SAUCE

Makes about 450 ml (¾ pint)

50 g (2 oz) plain chocolate
25 g (1 oz) butter
60 ml (4 tbsp) warm milk
225 g (8 oz) soft brown sugar
30 ml (2 tbsp) golden syrup
5 ml (1 tsp) vanilla flavouring

1 Break up the chocolate and put into a bowl standing over a saucepan of hot water. Add the butter. Leave until the chocolate and butter have melted, stirring once or twice.

2 Off the heat, blend in the milk and transfer the chocolate mixture to a saucepan. Add sugar and syrup.

3 Stir over a low heat until the sugar has dissolved. Bring to the boil and boil steadily without stirring for 5 minutes. Remove pan from heat. Add vanilla flavouring and mix well. Serve hot with ice cream, and steamed puddings.

BUTTERSCOTCH NUT SAUCE

Makes about 100 ml (4 fl oz)

25 g (1 oz) butter
30 ml (2 tbsp) brown sugar
15 ml (1 tbsp) golden syrup
45 ml (3 tbsp) chopped nuts
squeeze of lemon juice (optional)

1 Warm the butter, sugar and syrup in a saucepan until well blended. Boil for 1 minute and stir in the nuts and lemon juice.

JAM SAUCE

Makes about 225 ml (8 fl oz)

60 ml (4 tbsp) jam, sieved
150 ml (¼ pint) juice, drained from a can of fruit
10 ml (2 tsp) arrowroot
30 ml (2 tbsp) cold water
squeeze of lemon juice, optional

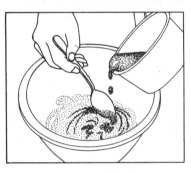

1 Warm the jam with the fruit juice and simmer gently for 5 minutes, stirring to blend well. Blend the arrowroot and cold water to a smooth cream and stir in the jam mixture.

2 Return to the pan and heat gently until it thickens and clears, stirring constantly. Add the lemon juice.

——— VARIATION ———

Thick jam sauce Omit the fruit juice and arrowroot. Heat the jam gently in a heavy-based saucepan until just melted and stir in a little lemon juice.

LEMON SAUCE

Makes about 350 ml (12 fl oz)

juice and grated rind of 1 large lemon
15 ml (1 tbsp) cornflour
30 ml (2 tbsp) sugar
knob of butter
1 egg yolk, optional

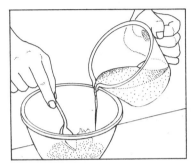

1 Make up the lemon juice to 300 ml (½ pint) with water. Add the lemon rind. Blend a little of the liquid with the cornflour and the sugar until smooth.

2 Bring the remaining liquid to the boil and stir into the creamed cornflour. Return all the liquid to the pan and bring to the boil, stirring until the sauce thickens and clears. Add butter.

3 Cool, beat in the egg yolk if used and reheat without boiling, stirring all the time.

——— VARIATION ———

Orange sauce Use the juice and rind of an orange instead of a lemon.

SYRUP SAUCE

Makes about 150 ml (¼ pint)

60–75 ml (4–5 tbsp) golden syrup
45 ml (3 tbsp) water
juice of ½ a lemon

1 Put the syrup and water in a saucepan, stir over gentle heat until blended, then simmer for 3–4 minutes. Add the lemon juice.

CINNAMON CREAM SAUCE

Makes 150 ml ($\frac{1}{4}$ pint)

150 ml (5 fl oz) single cream

5 ml (1 tsp) caster sugar

1.25 ml ($\frac{1}{4}$ tsp) ground cinnamon

Pour the cream into a bowl, stir in the sugar and cinnamon until evenly blended, then chill.

SOURED CREAM SAUCE

Makes 300 ml ($\frac{1}{2}$ pint)

30 ml (2 tbsp) custard powder

20 ml (4 tsp) soft light brown sugar

300 ml ($\frac{1}{2}$ pint) milk

142 ml (5 fl oz) soured cream

1 In a small bowl, mix the custard powder and the sugar to a smooth paste with a little of the milk.

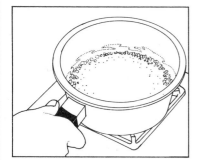

2 Scald the remaining milk and pour on to the custard mixture stirring well.

3 Return the custard to the pan and bring to the boil, stirring all the time and boil for 2–3 minutes. Lower the heat and carefully stir in the soured cream, then warm through without boiling.

SABAYON SAUCE

Makes about 150 ml ($\frac{1}{4}$ pint)

2 egg yolks

50 g (2 oz) caster sugar

pinch of arrowroot

100 ml (4 fl oz) sherry or white wine

1 Beat the egg yolks and sugar together until pale and creamy. Blend the arrowroot with the sherry or white wine and gradually whisk this into the egg and sugar mixture. Place the bowl over a pan of gently simmering water and whisk until thick and frothy. Serve at once.

COLD SABAYON SAUCE

Makes about 150 ml ($\frac{1}{4}$ pint)

50 g (2 oz) caster sugar

60 ml (4 tbsp) water

2 egg yolks, beaten

grated rind of $\frac{1}{2}$ a lemon

juice of 1 lemon

30 ml (2 tbsp) rum or sherry

30 ml (2 tbsp) single cream

1 Dissolve the sugar in the water and boil for 2–3 minutes, until syrupy. Pour slowly on to the yolks whisking until pale and thick. Add the lemon rind, lemon juice and rum or sherry and whisk for a further few minutes. Fold in the cream and chill well.

MOUSSELINE SAUCE

Makes about 150 ml ($\frac{1}{4}$ pint)

1 egg

1 egg yolk

45 ml (3 tbsp) sugar

15 ml (1 tbsp) sherry

60 ml (4 tbsp) single cream

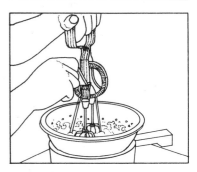

1 Place all the ingredients in a bowl over a pan of boiling water and whisk until pale and frothy and of a creamy thick consistency. Serve at once.

COFFEE CREAM SAUCE

Makes about 200 ml (7 fl oz)

10 ml (2 tsp) instant coffee powder

150 ml (5 fl oz) double cream

15 ml (1 tbsp) milk

30 ml (2 tbsp) caster sugar

vanilla flavouring

1 Dissolve the coffee powder in 10 ml (2 tsp) hot water. Cool slightly and mix in the cream, milk, sugar and a few drops of vanilla flavouring. Whisk until the cream begins to hold its shape.

INDEX